# DECORATING WITH FLOWERS

ULA PRYKE

# DECORATING WITH FLOWERS

CLASSIC AND CONTEMPORARY ARRANGEMENTS

RIZZOLI
NEW YORK
New York · Paris · London · Milan

In memory of our colleague and dear friend Natasha Tshoukas, February 11, 1986–March 31, 2009. A natural floral genius and a truly wonderful person.

First published in the United States of America in 2010 by Rizzoli International Publications, Inc.
300 Park Avenue South
New York, NY 10010
www.rizzoliusa.com

Originally published in the United Kingdom in 2010 as *The Ultimate Floral Collection* by Jacqui Small LLP,
7 Greenland Street
London NW1 0ND



2010 2011 2012 2013 /
10 9 8 7 6 5 4 3 2 1

ISBN: 978-0-8478-3429-7

Library of Congress Control Number: 2009936366

Printed in China

**Publisher** Jacqui Small
**Editorial Manager** Kerenza Swift
**Designer** Maggie Town
**Editor** Sian Parkhouse
**Production** Peter Colley

# contents

**OPPOSITE** I feel extremely privileged to be able to work professionally with flowers, and one of the motivating forces for me is working with color.

# my floral design vision

*To gild refined gold, to paint the lily . . . is wasteful and ridiculous excess.*

WILLIAM SHAKESPEARE

**in the mid-eighties** I changed my career from teaching history to floristry. In retrospect, I realize that flowers and plants have always been very central to my life, and when I was looking for a new career the lure of the flower industry was magnetic, and it has become an enduring passion. I think it is fair to say that in the eighties the flower industry in the United Kingdom was at a low point, and so as I eagerly picked up my grounding in floristry and flower arranging, I came to challenge some of the principles of practice that had become quite established at that time. I had no idea back in 1988 that by starting a small flower shop on a site in North London I would become one of the exponents of a radical new approach to commercial flower design and personal flower arranging.

Back then I only had an aspiration to work with beautiful flowers all day, creating attractive designs that would please the recipients. From those early days, while I didn't necessarily set out to be different, my bouquets and arrangements were so positively received that I realized we had established a new floral design aesthetic. Just three years into my new business venture I was offered the chance to write my first flower book, *The New Floral Artist*. Still in print and translated into several languages, this book brought my work to a much wider audience. It

became a portfolio of ideas for many flower shops across the world and established me as an international floral designer. I believe that the essence of being a good floral designer is to have empathy with nature and the ability to translate the desires of your customers and clients. At one level, this may be wrapping a single stem to woo a new love, or at the other end of the scale it may be an extravagant party where the clients' fantasies have been the inspiration for the floral design. This variety has led me to interpret many ideas and work in lots of different floral styles. My own personal style and preference is for natural, abundant, and romantic flowers. I prefer simple arrangements with a wild twist.

The designer Terence Conran, with whom I have had the pleasure of working for over twenty years, once described my work as "grand yet simple at the same time," and I could not put it better myself. I dislike overworked, fussy designs and prefer flowers to speak for themselves. I like to think that in my work the flowers are the stars. I hope my input enhances the beauty of the plant material without being too dominant, and that my style is accessible to all. Nature is the most impressive teacher and has been the most important creative force in my work. Inspiration may come from a flower, a leaf pattern, a tree shape, or the much wider landscape, like a woodland smothered in bluebells or an inspirational garden, such as the seventeenth-century topiaries of Levens Hall in the English Lake District. Nature has been a huge influence in my life and on my work.

Paula Pryke

# essential flower care

The fundamental requirement of all plant life is water and food, and supplying these needs in the right way, by mastering some basic techniques, ensures that your flowers will last as long as possible.

## equipment

To start off with, you only really need a good pair of scissors, a sharp knife, and some strong pruning shears. Next you will want some wire, blocks of floral foam, and pot tape. Changes in commercial floristry have meant a greater range of media is available, such as shells, fruits, vegetables, gravel, and products like donuts and test tubes. You can buy sundries from flower clubs or from wholesalers over the Internet.

## conditioning flowers

Re-cut the stems of all flowers and foliage and place them into a clean container. As a general rule, take ½ inch off the end of the stem, creating a slanted cut to allow maximum surface area. Bashing or cutting the flower ends vertically destroys valuable cell structure in the stem, causing some rot and bacteria, which in turn obstructs water absorption, so never do this. Flowers should never go into water that is too cold as lukewarm water provides more oxygen and is better for the longevity of the flower. Alkaline faucet water holds more oxygen than slightly acidic rainwater.

## feeding cut flowers

Once a flower has been cut from the plant, it does not have enough energy to breathe further. Many flowers are fed a postharvest solution to assist them on their journey from the grower to the end user. Many of these solutions contain sugars, such as glucose, to feed the flower and a disinfectant to prevent bacteria. This explains why household remedies for keeping flowers, such as adding bleach or sugar, have some credence.

## my top five tips

**1** Check the maturity of the flowers that you are purchasing and unwrap them as soon as you can.

**2** Cut the ends of the stems obliquely using a sharp knife or scissors. Remove any foliage that will fall under the water line and any that is not enhancing the flower.

**3** Clean buckets with household bleach or disinfectant. Then add clean lukewarm faucet water mixed with flower food added to the ratio indicated on the packet.

**4** Place the flowers in well-ventilated storage, preferably around 43°F and keep an eye on the water—a flower will drink a third of its water in the first 12 hours.

**5** Remove any damaged leaves or flowers, and make sure you do not store flowers near fruits and vegetables.

## special tips for certain flowers

Buy fresh flowers from reliable sources, or as close to the geographical grower as possible for longevity. Seasonal flowers are always the best purchase. Check the foliage and the stem to make sure they look fresh and strong and that they smell fresh. Take care that buds are not too green.

**1 Rose** Roses should be purchased when the bud is fully developed and showing color and has fresh leaves. Flower food is essential. Re-cut stems and refresh often with lukewarm water for maximum life. Remove thorns and lower foliage with a sharp knife without damaging the stem.

**2 Hyacinth** This wonderful scented spring bulb is usually cut just above the bulb, and it is vital to the strength of the stems to try to keep as much of the base on the stem as possible. Hyacinth bulbs are often cultivated in sandy soils, so rinse off any grains before using the flowers.

**3 Euphorbia** All euphorbias bleed when their stems are cut, exuding a milky latex substance. This is an irritant to skin and can cause inflammation if placed near the eyes. You can simply cut the ends of the stems and condition them in the normal way, but if you wish to use these flowers in a glass vase you can seal the ends. The best way to do this is to plunge them into boiling water for five seconds. While you are doing this protect the flower heads from the effects of the steam by wrapping them in paper.

**4 Poppy** Sadly, most poppies are short lived, both in their natural habitat and as cut flowers. *Papaver nudicaule* last between six and nine days. Most poppies are supplied with singed stems because they exude a milky sap. If you need to trim them, it is essential that you resinge them with a naked flame. Oriental and *somniferum* varieties generally last about four days, but they are useful for their long-lasting seed heads, which can be used green or dried in arrangements or Christmas decorations.

**5 Hippeastrum** The best way to condition these is to trim an inch from the end of the stem and then insert a bamboo cane to protect the head while the stem takes water to the flower head. Most amaryllis have four heads and they take over a week to open fully. These flowers have been heavily hybridized, so the head is very large. The cane in the hollow stem helps to support the stem when the flower is fully extended.

4

3

5

# colorful creations

OPPOSITE A cube filled with colored gravel is topped with a mixed bouquet of purple phlox, pink *Ozothamnus diosmifolius*, nepenthes, *Gomphocarpus physocarpus* 'Moby Dick', *Rosa* 'Vampire' and 'Shadow', and striped 'Sunlife' calla lilies.

**color is without doubt** one of the most motivating forces in my work and my life. I adore color, and over the years vibrant color schemes have been a trademark of my flower style. It is such a pleasure each day to work with the colors of nature, and the infinite variety the natural palette offers is astonishing. The constant interaction of nature and humankind to create new varieties means that these color options evolve all the time and bring fresh inspiration to seasonal designs.

Some people have a natural flair for color, and others find it harder to make good color combinations. Color is of course a matter of taste, but those who don't feel confident choosing colors usually start by studying the color wheel. In my view, any color can be made to work with another color with the right combination of texture and foliage. I think this theory is borne out by the pages of this book, where many unharmonious combinations can, in my opinion, offer perfect harmony.

As a florist, it is important to understand how to use color to convey a feeling and to make an attractive gift. Professional florists usually work with the color preferences of their clients, and sometimes this is the first requirement even before a budget has been set or a flower variety specifed. Color is often the first thing on our minds when we are planning to send a gift to a friend. We use the words vibrant, clashing, calm, pale, clean, minimal, or sophisticated to conjure up the kind of floral color combination we want. When we are thinking of flowers for our home we use color to enhance the room or mood or reflect the season. When we choose our wedding or party flowers, color is very often the first consideration.

# green flowers

GREEN IS THE DOMINANT COLOR in the landscape and is restful and pleasing. For me it is the alchemist of the color spectrum, because it allows me to transform other colors. It acts like an elixir in my hands. Flower arrangers know only too well the power of green. Spires of *Moluccella* are thought almost essential for large arrangements, and fluffy fillers such as *Alchemilla mollis* are highly coveted for smaller decorations. Lime green flowers enhance color schemes by making them brighter and fresher, as well as looking great massed on their own.

**1 Alchemilla mollis** The vibrant tones of the delicate flowers are ideal for lifting adjacent flower colors.

**2 Fountain grass** Grasses have become very popular in both garden borders and flower arrangements.

**3 Hydrangea** Large, long-lasting flowers, some of which emerge green before turning pink or blue.

**4 Gladiolus** Sometimes known as the sword lily. Cut off the top bud to encourage the lower buds to open.

**5 Carnation** This cultivated *Dianthus carophyllus* 'Prado' is naturally green rather than dyed.

**6 Cymbidium orchids** With a long vase life, these exotic flowers offer extremely good value.

**7 Hellebore** The delicate green shading of the petals deepens at the central core.

OPPOSITE This 'Green Shamrock' chrysanthemum is perfect for adding a shot of vibrant, concentrated lime green to a bouquet.

Everybody loves green and it is always seen as sophisticated and chic. It is soothing and it suits all interiors, so it is the most popular choice for people when sending flowers. Mixed with white, it remains the number-one favorite color scheme for weddings.

# green arrangements

LEFT A glass bowl lined with stems of pussy willow is filled with a selection of fresh spring flowers and foliage: *Brachyglottis* 'Sunshine', *Viburnum opulus* (guelder rose), ranunculus, anemones, and white roses.

OPPOSITE This vibrant arrangement will stand up to the intense light levels of high summer. Delphiniums, calla lilies, 'Avalanche+' roses, 'Pompei' lilies, *Viburnum opulus* 'Roseum', *Moluccella*, *Syringa* 'Madame Florent Stepman', larkspur, antirrhinums, and lime green kangaroo paw (*Anigozanthos flavidus*) are set off with a collar of trailing smilax (*Asparagus asparagoides*).

OPPOSITE To create a candle centerpiece, foam is placed in a lined terra-cotta pot. Lichen-covered twigs, skimmia, hypericum, eucalyptus, *Viburnum tinus* berries and flowers, and contorted willow were added, and finally twenty small-headed 'Akito' roses.

RIGHT Cymbidium orchids normally dominate an arrangement because they are visually arresting. The folded pandanus leaves change the balance within the arrangement.

BELOW Grouped viburnum berries, variegated *Viburnum tinus*, hypericum, camellia, kale, and a little eucalyptus for scent are enclosed in a folded collar of glossy, curled aspidistra leaves.

RIGHT For a winter centerpiece, a wreath frame was placed around a glass bowl filled with water and floating candles. Groups of tulips, lilac, guelder roses, *Brunia laevis*, and green and white hellebores have been placed in the wreath.

LEFT Men often respond to exotic plants and sculptural shapes. *Phormium tenax* 'Variegatum', *Nelumbo*, *Hypericum androsaemum* 'Jade Flair', *Tillandsia*, and 'Maureen' tulips form a masculine-feeling bouquet.

OPPOSITE This bright and cheerful spring arrangement of lilac, camellia, *Viburnum opulus*, ivy berries, and *Helleborus foetidus*, with pale cream Clooney ranunculus and scented cream *Narcissi*, is augmented by branches of catkins. This verdant display is balanced by the verdigris effect of the urn.

# green is good with . . .

Green is an excellent companion to all colors. Lime green flowers work well with all combinations, adding freshness and light to dark or vibrant arrangements. I am wary of variegated foliage greens, which I tend to use only in winter when flower choice is limited.

## . . . purple

ABOVE This oval glass vase holds a hand-tied bouquet of green and pink hellebores, forget-me-nots, and deep purple flag irises. It could easily be presented as a gift.

## . . . mixed colors

This harmonious vase combines delphiniums, peony tulips, lilac, guelder roses, 'Green Shamrock' chrysanthemums, eustoma, and Solomon's seal.

## green is good with . . . contrasting colors

OPPOSITE Matching orange 'Wow' roses, bright orange germini gerberas, and textural orange leucospermum have been contrasted with green ivy berries, 'Lemon and Lime' roses, and 'Jade' hypericum.

ABOVE Small posies of 'Cherry Brandy' roses, green 'Prado' carnations, *Alchemilla mollis*, and *Asclepias* have been placed in glass tumblers lined with asparagus spears.

# white flowers

WHITE IS THE COLOR WE OFTEN choose to mark our most intense and serious occasions. Its long associations with purity and integrity have meant that it is the number-one flower for weddings and civil ceremonies. It is the most popular choice for that all-important wedding bouquet, with lily of the valley, sweet peas, peonies, roses, orchids, and calla lilies being the current white favorites. It is the safe color we turn to when sending a gift to an acquaintance, because white flowers are seen as chic and sophisticated and always in style.

**1 Snowflake** Larger than the common snowdrop, *Leucojum* 'Spring Snowflake' flowers in the spring.

**2 Amaryllis** Highly valued as a cut flower, *Hippeastrum* 'Mont Blanc' has an impressive vase life.

**3 Freesia** Popular as much for its wonderful scent as for its purity of color and pretty flowers.

**4 Hellebore** Cup-shaped flowers, some with speckled markings, which make pretty small posies.

**5 Tulip** The white 'Maureen' has a wonderful clean color—use it grouped or massed for best effect.

**6 Pussy willow** Malleable stems of *Salix* are wonderful for lining glass vases, adding horizontal interest.

**7 Snowberry** Ideal for weddings, these pink-tinged waxy fruits add shape and texture to arrangements.

OPPOSITE Good for wedding bouquets and displaying in single vases as cut stems, phalaenopsis orchids also make great pot plants.

## winter whites

1 *Hippeastrum* 'Ludwig Dazzler' (amaryllis) 2 *Euphorbia fulgens* 'Largo White' 3 *Rosa* 'Avalanche' 4 *Brassica oleracea* 'Corgy White' (ornamental kale) 5 *Chamelaucium uncinatum* 'Blondie' (Geraldton wax) 6 *Lilium longiflorum* 'White Europe' (Easter lily) 7 *Brunia albiflora* 8 *Dahlia* 'Karma Serena' 9 *Gladiolus* 'Mont Blanc' 10 *Gossypium herbaceum* (levant cotton) 11 *Genista* 12 *Eucharis amazonica* 13 *Syringa vulgaris* 'Primrose' (lilac) 14 *Hyacinthus orientalis* 'Mont Blanc' (hyacinth) 15 *Ranunculus* 'Ranobelle Inra White' 16 *Narcissus tazetta* 'Ziva' 17 *Lilium* 'Casa Blanca' 18 *Phalaenopsis* 'Alpha' 19 *Gypsophila* 'Lucky Stars' 20 *Hydrangea arborescens* 'Annabelle' 21 *Anthurium* 'Bianca'

## all-year-round whites

1 *Zantedeschia aethiopica* 'Colombe de la Paix' (arum lily, calla lily) 2 *Eucharis amazonica* 3 *Brachyglottis* 'Sunshine' (senecio) 4 *Aster novi-belgii* 'M. C. Snowy' (Michaelmas daisy) 5 *Chrysanthemum* 'Reagan White' 6 *Eustoma grandiflorum* 'Alice White' (lisianthus) 7 *Freesia* 'Alaska' 8 *Ornithogalum thyrsoides* 'Mount Fuji' (chincherinchee) 9 *Hypericum androsaemum* 'King Flair' (tutsan) 10 *Rosmarinus officinalis* (rosemary) 11 *Dendrobium* 'Madame Pompadour White' 12 *Rosa* 'Iceberg' 13 *Rosa* 'Akito' 14 *Gerbera jamesonii* 'Bianca' (Barbarton daisy) 15 *Lilium longiflorum* 'Snow Queen' (Easter lily) 16 *Stephanotis floribunda* (bridal wreath, Madagascar jasmine) 17 *Cymbidium* 'R. B. Mieke' 18 *Anthurium* 'Captain' 19 *Dianthus* 'Dover' (carnation) 20 *Gypsophila* 'Little White'

The winter months are when I feel most in tune with white. The landscape is barren and I enjoy white more because there are fewer colors to distract me. I particularly turn to white after the colorful excesses of the festive season and for the start of the new year.

# white arrangements

LEFT Miniature green limequats sit in a round glass wreath vase filled with water, topped with five perfect gardenia flowers and white floating candles.

OPPOSITE Shot glasses in a ring make a simple centerpiece when filled with posies of snowflakes and sprigs of jasmine, wrapped in hydrangea leaves. Twisted decorative florists' wire has been gently wound around the flower stems for added visual interest.

OPPOSITE Rare white spathiphyllum flowers from Holland have been teamed with pussy willow to make a round cage. Set in a low frosted dish with floral foam concealed by white sand, the pussy willow has been shaped into a ball.

RIGHT A small tied posy of tight 'Margaret Merril' rosebuds bound with silk and a pearl prom corsage bracelet makes a stunning bridal bouquet.

LEFT White phalaenopsis orchids have been hand tied with three small *Monstera* leaves and then placed in an elegant frosted vase. The proportion of these delicate arching flowers perfectly complements the tall vase.

This living topiary is comprised of seven white amaryllis stems tied beneath their flower heads and at the base of their stems, arranged in a frosted glass vase with a collar of white lilac. The white container reinforces the monochromatic harmony of this design.

White scabious, some garden roses, large heads of white hydrangea, poppy seed heads, *Alchemilla mollis*, *Ammi visnaga*, and some stems of fruiting ivy berries top a glass vase filled with small green apples.

I used a bowl-shaped twig basket for this centerpiece, filling the middle with pots of fragrant paperwhite *Narcissi* overlaid with trailing jasmine and groups of small shiny pearl baubles. Silver lanterns and more jasmine trails continue the theme on the rest of the table.

Chunky ornamental kales, 'Avalanche+' roses, and white cymbidium orchids are softened with the addition of lilac and ruscus. Jasmine and stephanotis make this a fabulously scented combination.

# white is good with . . .

On the surface, white appears to work well with all flower colors, but I prefer it with pastels, such as pink, or with yellows, blues, and creams. It looks sublime with green—the best companion color for white if it is not being used en masse in a monochromatic scheme.

## . . . blue and yellow

OPPOSITE Tiny bouquets of *Muscari* 'Bluefields Beauty', *Viola*, *Narcissus* 'Carlton', *Narcissus* 'Geranium', and snowflake look great individually, and even nicer grouped in a ring.

## . . . green

The delicate white flowers of eucharis and jasmine in this simple hand-tied bouquet contrast with some hebe, *Garrya elliptica*, and one of my favorite textural foliages, *Brachyglottis* 'Sunshine'.

# blue flowers

THE SPECTRUM OF BLUE FLOWERS is wide, from the palest lilac to the deepest navy blue. Pale blue, purple, and lilac flowers become plentiful in spring as bulb flowers, such as anemones, tulips, hyacinths, *Muscari*, irises, and scillas, come into season. In early summer, there are scented sweet peas and branches of fragrant lilac, followed by dainty cottage garden favorites, such as nigella, cornflowers, and the spiky eryngiums and echinops. The big season for blue for me is really midsummer, when the delphiniums and agapanthus are standing tall in the border.

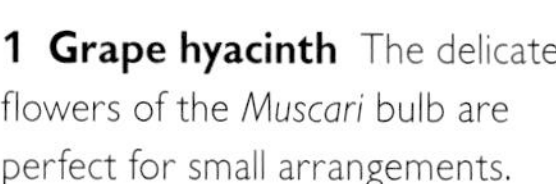

**1 Grape hyacinth** The delicate flowers of the *Muscari* bulb are perfect for small arrangements.

**2 Aconitum** This stunning flower is highly poisonous, so take care when handling it—wear rubber gloves.

**3 Scabious** Open, ruffled flowers look stunning in hand-tied bouquets, giving a "country garden" feel.

**4 Eustoma** Delicate, bell-shaped, flowers, also known as lisianthus, give movement to arrangements.

**5 Lilac** Beautiful, versatile, and often scented, the large trusses of flowers are ideal for hand-tied bouquets.

**6 Hyacinth** The bells of *Hyacinthus orientalis* 'Delft Blue' are perfect for pipping and wiring together.

**7 Triteleia** The pretty flowers of this early summer flowering bulb have a distinctive starry shape.

OPPOSITE Irises don't have great stamina, so try to arrange them in water rather than foam so they maintain their glorious color.

## spring blues

1 *Delphinium* 'Skyline' 2 *Agapanthus* 'Donau' 3 *Consolida ajacis* 'Sydney Purple' (larkspur) 4 *Delphinium* Belladonna Group 'Völkerfrieden' 5 *Liatris spicata* 'Blue Bird' (gayfeather) 6 *Veronica longifolia* 'Blauriesen' 7 *Delphinium* Belladonna Group 'Sky Lady' 8 *Freesia* 'Côte d'Azur' 9 *Matthiola incana* 'Arabella' (stock) 10 *Tulipa* 'Black Parrot' 11 *Iris* 'Purple Rain' 12 *Lathyrus odoratus* (sweet pea) 13 *Aquilegia* 'Blue Lady' (columbine) 14 *Scilla siberica* (Siberian squill) 15 *Myosotis sylvatica* (forget-me-not) 16 *Hyacinthus orientalis* 'Delft Blue' (hyacinth) 17 *Muscari armeniacum* 'Blue Dream' (grape hyacinth) 18 *Anemone coronaria* 'Galil Purper' 19 *Anemone coronaria* 'Marianne Blue' 20 *Matthiola incana* 'Lucinda Purple' (stock) 21 *Syringa* x *hyacinthiflora* 'Esther Staley' (lilac) 22 *Trachelium caeruleum* 'Blue Wonder' (blue throatwort) 23 *Syringa vulgaris* 'Andenken an Ludwig Spaeth' (lilac)

## summer blues

1 *Gentiana* 'Sky' (gentian) 2 *Delphinium* Belladonna Group 'Blue Shadow' 3 *Rosa* 'Blue Moon' 4 *Ageratum houstonianum* 'Blue Horizon' 5 *Centaurea montana* (knapweed) 6 *Scabiosa stellata* 'Ping Pong' (pincushion flower, scabious) 7 *Lathyrus odoratus* 'Lila' (sweet pea) 8 *Cotinus coggygria* 'Royal Purple' (smoke bush) 9 *Zantedeschia* 'Anneke' (arum lily, calla lily) 10 *Delphinium* 'Faust' 11 *Allium sphaerocephalon* 12 *Delphinium* 'Lilac Arrow' 13 *Hydrangea macrophylla* 'Blue' 14 *Scabiosa caucasica* 'Clive Greaves' (pincushion flower, scabious) 15 *Rosa* 'Blue Gene' 16 *Delphinium* 'Skyline'

Blue is essentially viewed as a masculine color and is always popular for clubs, companies, and business organizations. Many blue flowers are textural, such as echinops, eryngium, and nigella, and they are a versatile addition to many different designs.

# blue arrangements

LEFT If you find you have a lot of one particular flower, a single-variety wreath is an effective way of making good use of them. This arrangement is made from the heads of 'Supernova' Questar eryngium pushed into a floral-foam ring.

OPPOSITE A classic wood and metal urn holds a formal arrangement of predominantly blue midsummer flowers. *Brachyglottis* 'Sunshine' and *Alchemilla mollis* combine with hydrangea, sweet peas, astilbe, nigella, and some garden roses.

Repeated bunches of grape hyacinths and bluebells in glass fishbowl vases are echoed by smaller arrangements of grape hyacinths only. Crushed clear cellophane and lengths of flexigrass (*Xanthorrhoea australis*) add visual interest.

LEFT A bouquet of sweet peas, hyacinths, and *Triteleia* is dotted with the flowering heads of *Stachys byzantina*, with its felted gray foliage. The pot has been lined with stems of lavender, fixed with double-sided tape and held in place with twine.

OPPOSITE This scented door wreath has been designed on a foam ring with a base of *Brachyglottis* and *Viburnum tinus* berries, with groups of eucalyptus pods, hellebores, purple anemones, and clusters of *Gypsophila*. Bunches of dried lavender have been wired into the wreath to give texture and a great scent.

OPPOSITE Double-sided tape was wrapped around a glass vase and *Stachys byzantina* leaves were attached and tied with cord. Posies of sweet peas, *Triteleia*, marguerite daisies, white nigella, forget-me-nots, and *Origanum* 'Gijsie' have been placed in the vase.

RIGHT This stunning, tall arrangement would suit a large event. To make it, use two glass cubes of different sizes, with the space between them filled with blue and white sand. Long stems of *Agapanthus* 'Donau' are edged with flowering *Eucalyptus perriniana.*

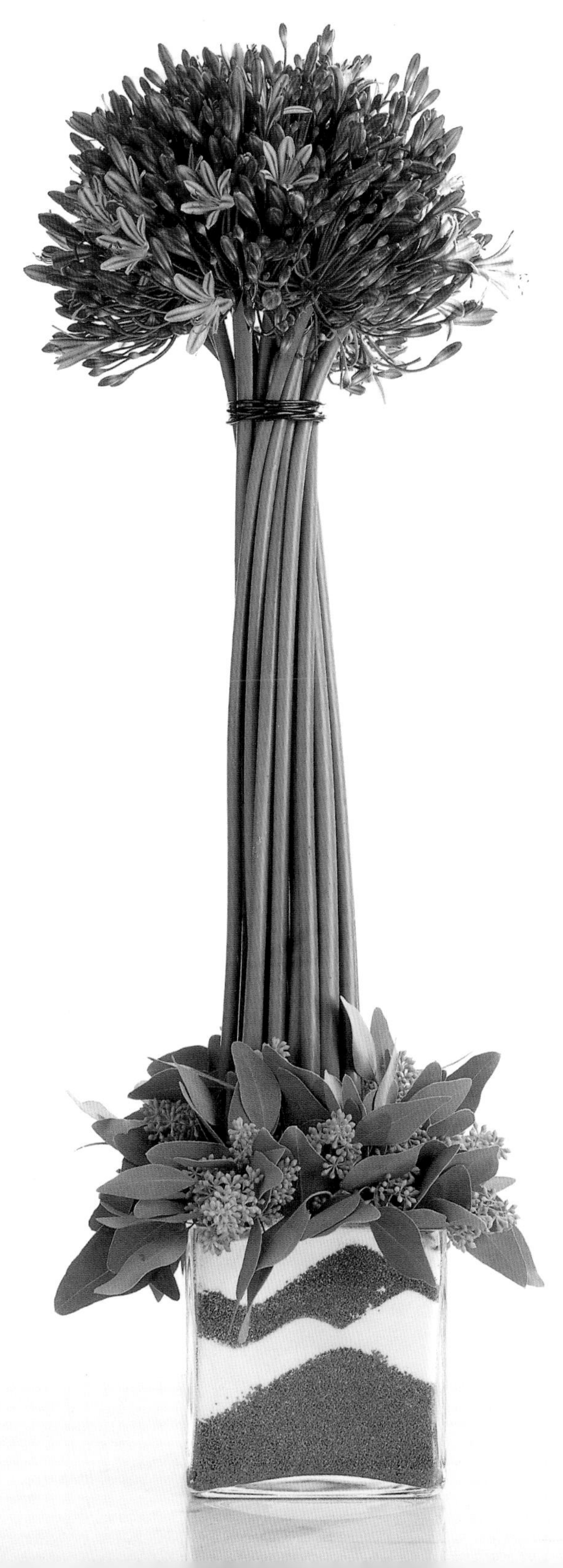

LEFT Deep blue hydrangea heads are massed tightly together in a dome shape on top of a clear glass cube filled with fine white sand.

OPPOSITE In this color-themed arrangement, blue hydrangea, blue scabious, blue echinops, and blue nigella have been mixed with white hydrangea, white dahlias, green *Alchemilla mollis*, green sedum, and some nigella seed heads.

A long, low silver and glass trough has been filled with four individual posies of dill, scabious, echinops, cornflower, ivy berries, and that indispensable summer filler plant, *Alchemilla mollis*.

# blue is good with . . .

Blues and purples work well with most other colors. Blue and white is quite crisp and is often chosen for church flowers and summer weddings. I think the mid and light blues of spring look great with primrose yellow or even the harsher yellows of *Narcissi* and forsythia.

## . . . yellow

ABOVE A mossed wreath has been decorated with potted primroses, blue hyacinths, and *Narcissi*. Twisted hazel stems have been worked through the wreath to add movement.

## . . . red and purple

Forget-me-nots, soft blue lilac, lime green guelder roses, deep purple anemones, hot pink gloriosa, and 'Milano' roses make this an analogous harmony of different colors.

## blue is good with . . . . . . pink

A pink enameled watering can holds blue and pink love-in-a-mist (*Nigella* 'Pink Power'), *Astilbe* 'Erica', pale pink stocks, pale lilac scabious, and double daisy *Aster* 'Pink Pearl'.

## . . . red and green

The soft green flower heads of *Lagurus* grass, red thistle flower heads, and astrantia form a counterpoint to the densely massed scabious, sweet peas, veronica, and roses.

# pink flowers

PINK IS MY FAVORITE COLOR, and many pink flower varieties are on my most desirable list, including ranunculus, sweet peas, peonies, and garden roses, such as 'Constance Spry' or 'Gertrude Jekyll', to name just a few. Pink is a diverse color. The palette is enormous, from shy pinks to in-your-face shocking pinks. There is a vast choice for the flower arranger, as so many flowers have been hybridized to include some varieties in the pink spectrum. It is certainly the most widely available color throughout the year, with most flowers available in an assortment of pink colors.

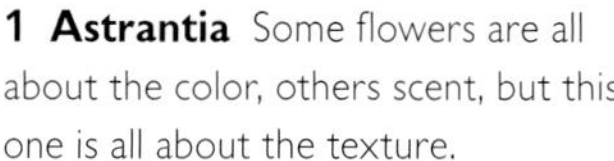

**1 Astrantia** Some flowers are all about the color, others scent, but this one is all about the texture.

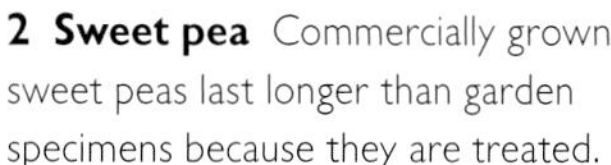

**2 Sweet pea** Commercially grown sweet peas last longer than garden specimens because they are treated.

**3 Clematis** These flowers are lovely for wedding work and trailing over the edge of vases and baskets.

**4 Nigella** This exciting new variety of the cottage garden favorite is appropriately called 'Power Pink'.

**5 Foxglove** I grow these in my garden and make the most of the supply when they are in season.

**6 Anthurium** These funny looking waxy flowers usually divide people into the love or hate camp!

**7 Valerian** I have come to adore these delicate flowers as fillers in bouquets and vase arrangements.

OPPOSITE There is a huge variety of pink tulips. Tulips continue to grow after they are cut, so allow for this when mixing with other flowers.

**1 Rhododendron** For a short season in spring, I love to use flowers from these magnificent shrubs.

**2 Celosia** The vivid color and lovely texture provide interest in densely packed arrangements.

**3 Peony** These quintessential blowsy, showy pink flowers have the added advantage of fragrance.

**4 Gerbera** You can buy these daisy-like flowers in any shade of pink just about any time of the year.

**5 Fuchsia** These have so aptly left their mark on the color pink by defining one of its best palettes.

**6 Dianthus** These old-fashioned, hard-working cottage garden "pinks" have a divine scent.

**7 Phalaenopsis orchid** Beautiful moth-shaped flower heads in a huge spectrum of bright pink color.

# spring pinks

1 *Eucalyptus ficifolia* 2 *Rosa* 'Aqua' 3 *Camellia* x *williamsii* 'E. G. Waterhouse' 4 *Rosa* 'Milano' 5 *Anemone coronaria* 'Mona Lisa Pink' 6 *Tulipa* 'Upstar' 7 *Lathyrus odoratus* (sweet pea) 8 *Tulipa* 'Lucky Strike' 9 *Hyacinthus orientalis* 'Anna Marie' (hyacinth) 10 *Paeonia* 'Sarah Bernhardt' 11 *Paeonia* 'Bowl of Beauty' 12 *Eustoma grandiflorum* 'Moon Pink' (lisianthus) 13 *Chamelaucium uncinatum* 'Wendy Rose' (Geraldton wax) 14 *Phlox* 'Bright Eyes' 15 *Rosa* 'Laminuette' 16 *Tulipa* 'Salmon Parrot' 17 *Gerbera germini* 'Sonate' 18 *Chaenomeles japonica* (flowering quince) 19 *Gladiolus* 'Priscilla' 20 *Prunus serrulata* 21 *Ranunculus* 'Ranobelle Inra' (dark pink) 22 *Ranunculus* 'Ranobelle Inra' (light pink) 23 *Antirrhinum majus* 'Potomac Red' (snapdragon)

## summer pinks

1 *Viburnum opulus* (guelder rose) 2 *Dahlia* 'Bicolor Karma' 3 *Rosa* 'Extase' 4 *Rosa* 'Jacaranda' 5 *Dianthus barbatus* 'Monarch Series' (sweet William) 6 *Gerbera* 'Dark Serena' 7 *Cirsium japonicum* 'Pink Beauty' 8 *Celosia argentea* var. *cristata* Cristata Group 'Bombay Pink' (cockscomb) 9 *Moluccella laevis* (bells of Ireland) 10 *Consolida ajacis* 'Sydney Rose' (larkspur) 11 *Paeonia lactiflora* 'Karl Rosenfield' 12 *Sorbus aria* 'Lutescens' (whitebeam) 13 *Lathyrus odoratus* (sweet pea) 14 *Rosa* 'Milano' 15 *Astilbe* x *arendsii* 'Erika' 16 *Eustoma grandiflorum* 'Mariachi Pink' (lisianthus) 17 *Rosa* 'Saint Celia' 18 *Crataegus laevigata* 'Paul's Scarlet' (may, hawthorn) 19 *Protea nerifolia* 20 *Lilium* 'Red Sox' 21 *Celosia argentea* var. *cristata* Plumosa Group 'Bombay Fire'

# fall pinks

1 *Symphoricarpos* x *doorenbosii* 'White Hedge' (snowberry) 2 *Astilbe* x *arendsii* 'Amerika' 3 *Symphoricarpos* 'Pink Pearl' (snowberry) 4 *Panicum miliaceum* (millet) 5 *Gerbera germini* 'Leila' 6 *Bouvardia* 'Bridesmaid' 7 *Rosa* 'Jacaranda' 8 *Rosa* 'Aqua' 9 *Rosa* 'Duo Unique' 10 *Sedum telephium* 'Mohrchen' 11 *Cirsium japonicum* 'Pink Beauty' 12 *Rosa* 'Mimi Eden' 13 *Rosa* 'Illusion' 14 *Celosia argentea* var. *cristata* Cristata Group 'Bombay Rose' 15 *Alchemilla mollis* (lady's mantle) 16 *Dahlia* 'Karma Thalia' 17 *Zantedeschia* 'Fantail Candy' (arum lily, calla lily)

Pink flowers are often associated with femininity, but recently, deeper and louder pink shades have enjoyed a wider audience. They are popular in vibrant mixes for bouquets and arrangements, and also for events. Small baskets and posies of pink flowers are carried by flower girls and bridesmaids the world over.

# pink arrangements

LEFT A striped glass Aline Johnson handkerchief vase is filled with pink waterlilies. As well as being a beautiful object in its own right, the vase's shape is perfect for displaying flowers.

OPPOSITE This brightly toned woven basket is filled with *Viburnum opulus* 'Roseum', asters, and 'Cristian' spray roses. This is an ideal gift to take with you if you are arriving at an event, as the hostess needs to do nothing other than display it and admire it!

OPPOSITE A bright pink glass cube vase holds a hand-tied bouquet of 'Milano' roses, *Alchemilla mollis*, echinops, gloriosa, *Brachyglottis* 'Sunshine' foliage, pink 'Karma Prospero', dark 'Karma Choc' dahlias, and peonies.

LEFT A big "basketball" sphere of green floral foam was placed on the top of a slightly flared cylinder vase, and then tightly covered with pale to mid-pink 'Heaven', 'Barbie', 'Blushing Akito', 'Video', and cream 'Talea+' roses.

ABOVE This ribbon-bound vase is filled with *Stephanandra*, *Cotinus coggygria* 'Royal Purple', *Lilium* 'Medusa', *Paeonia lactifolium* 'Karl Rosenfield', trailing amaranthus, *Dahlia* 'Karma Choc', and the small *Allium sphaerocephalon*.

Pale pink 'Gerrie Hoek' dahlias, 'Bridal Kimsey' gerberas, and 'Luxuria!' roses, interspersed with taper candles, are massed on a base of foam, edged with galax leaves secured with aluminum wire.

Here, 'Sarah Bernhardt' peonies are hand tied with brown 'Amnésia', pale pink 'Sweet Avalanche+', and dusty pink 'Two Faces+' roses, poppy seed heads, photinia, *Alchemilla mollis*, and green dill *Anethum graveolens*. Pink dye gives the water a rosy glow.

LEFT Tall spires of pale pink *Eremurus* rise from a lower layer of pink 'Amalia', 'Two Faces+', and 'Blushing Akito' roses, supported in a bright pink glass cube vase.

RIGHT A group of white mugs—the type that most of us have in our kitchen cabinet— looks stunning when filled with hand-tied posies of multihued sweet William.

# pink is good with . . .

Pink can be made more sophisticated by adding burgundy foliage and deep red flowers, or it can be made more vibrant by adding orange and green. The palest pink can look very girly, but it can also be very stylish, particularly in the right setting and in good daylight.

## . . . blues

BELOW A round wreath to be worn on the crown of the head has been made from variegated ivy leaves, pips of tuberosa, pink ranunculus, and *Muscari*.

## . . . greens

This large, glossy pink urn is filled with pink rhododendron, hydrangea, white lilac, spiraea, gladioli, larkspur, hanging amaranthus, dicentra, peonies, and the green-flowered guelder rose *Viburnum opulus* 'Roseum'.

## pink is good with . . . contrasting colors

ABOVE Wired seashells stud a spiraled hand-tied posy of green amaranthus, blue 'Whisper' eryngiums, germini gerberas, *Alchemilla mollis*, garden roses, and a collar of coral fern *Gleichenia polypodioides*.

OPPOSITE A dome of 'Revival', 'Prima Donna', and 'Ilios!' roses, veronica, 'Gipsy Queen' hyacinths, and green amaranthus. The green balls are *Linum usitatissimum*, grown mostly for dried flower supply.

# red flowers

THE MOST POPULAR TIMES for red flowers are for romantic occasions and the festive season. The romantic symbolism of red roses means that these are in constant demand and to be found on every florist's stock list. For Valentine's Day the requirement is so great the price shoots sky-high. I would say red roses are a bit of a Friday night staple; a conventional token, traditional but still symbolic. Personally I am most drawn to red in the winter months when the bleak weather and short length of daylight make you yearn for color and warmth.

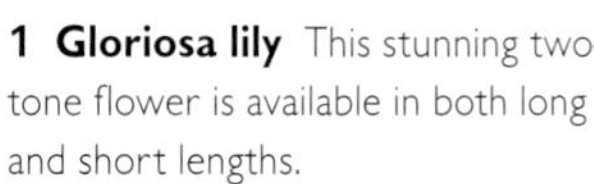

**1 Gloriosa lily** This stunning two-tone flower is available in both long and short lengths.

**2 Zinnia** Large, daisy-shaped dazzling flowers that give a retro and fun feel to hand-tied bouquets.

**3 Tulip** Small waxy spring flower in a huge range of colors and varieties, including fringed and parrot.

**4 Rose hip** Fall berries bring texture and a seasonal feel; use them to create a collar around vase tops.

**5 Dahlia** Long-stemmed summer flowers in a range of colors, shapes, and sizes, including bright red.

**6 Chrysanthemum** Versatile and long-lasting—up to three weeks if you change the water regularly.

**7 Rose** The red rose is enduringly popular, especially for Valentine's Day, and 'Grand Prix' is a classic.

OPPOSITE To help amaryllis bear the weight of the large open flower heads, you can insert a bamboo cane into the hollow stems.

## winter reds

OPPOSITE The deep tones of red peonies demonstrate the power of this vibrant color.

1 *Gladiolus* 'Addi' 2 *Capsicum annuum* (pepper) 3 *Anemone* 'Mona Lisa Red' 4 *Rosa canina* (dog rose, common briar) 5 *Hippeastrum* 'Red Lion' (amaryllis) 6 *Photinia* x *fraseri* 'Red Robin' 7 *Ilex verticillata* 'Oosterwijk' (winterberry) 8 *Gerbera germini* 'Salsa' 9 *Rosa* 'Grand Prix' 10 *Callistemon citrinus* (crimson bottlebrush) 11 *Chrysanthemum* 'Reagan Red' 12 *Skimmia japonica* 'Rubella' 13 *Leucadendron* 'Safari Sunset' 14 *Chrysanthemum* 'Early Bird Red' 15 *Tulipa* 'Prominence' 16 *Anthurium* 'Choco' (flamingo flower) 17 *Rosa* 'Black Baccara' 18 *Ranunculus* 'Pauline Scarlet' 19 *Gerbera germini* 'Midnight' 20 *Alpinia purpurata* (red ginger)

The velvet texture and the smoky red hues make these darkest of flowers the most prized possessions in a bouquet. One reason for their success is their main role in supporting other colors. In my opinion this is their true worth and where they do their magic.

# red arrangements

LEFT A straight-sided glass bowl has been filled with red dogwood, floral foam, and then ivy berries and red skimmia, followed by 'Naomi' and 'Black Baccara' roses, red Clooney ranunculus, and 'Ronaldo' tulips. Red petals have been scattered on the marble table to extend the display.

OPPOSITE A similar treatment was given to this bowl; here the layers of dogwood stems are topped with waxed red apples, ranunculus, *Viburnum tinus* berries, fruiting ivy, red 'Grand Prix' roses dyed black, and black dahlias.

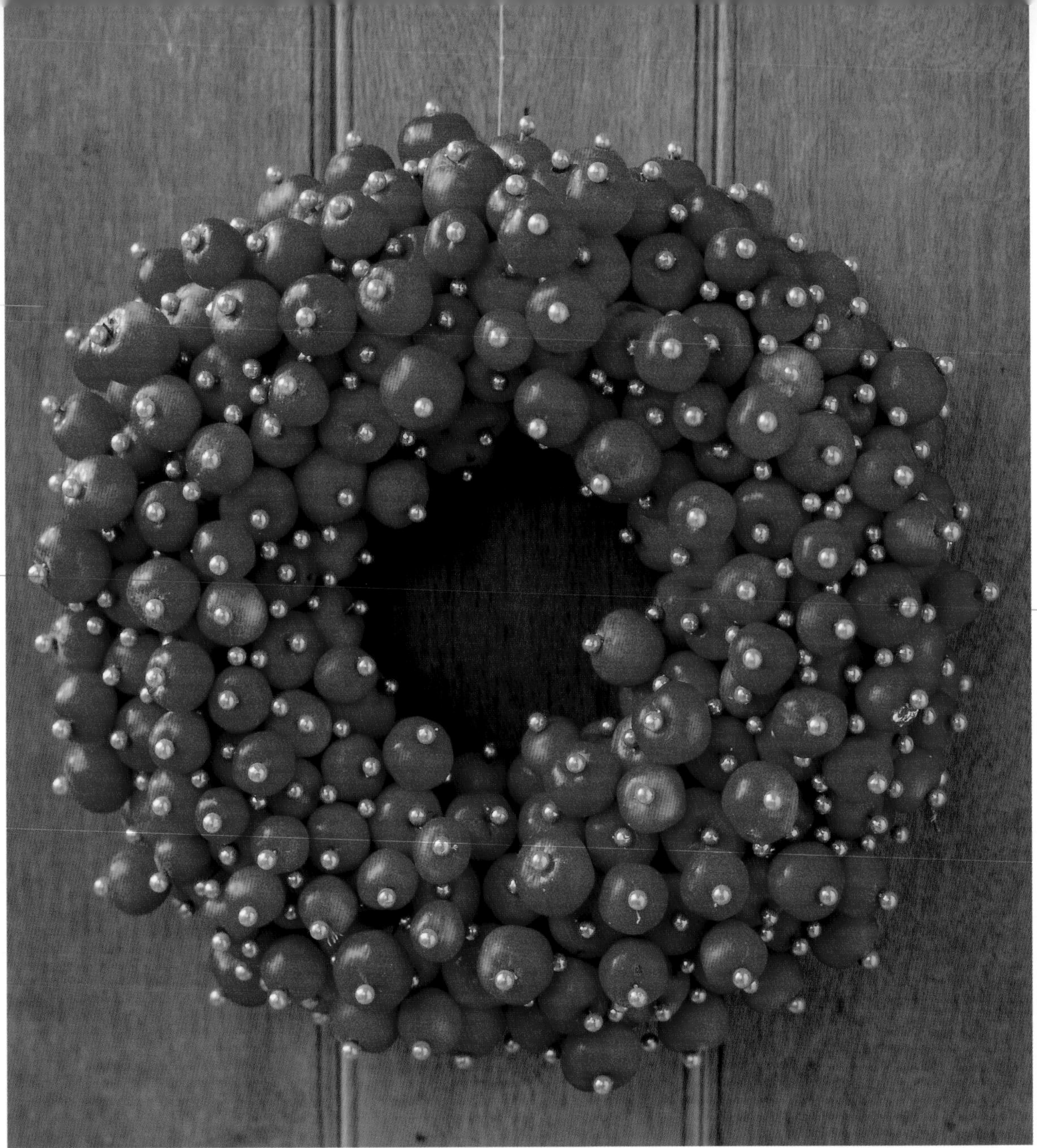

ABOVE Some of the most effective wreaths feature just one element, in this case around two hundred tiny red crab apples topped with pearlized green bead-headed pins.

OPPOSITE A mixture of orange roses was hand tied with amaranthus, hypericum, cotoneaster, and *Euphorbia fulgens* and placed in a round bowl filled with crab apples to make a fall table display.

A group of red glass vases in varying heights is filled with posies of 'Passion' roses and foliage, skimmia, and, in the tallest display, some rose hips.

Red roses studded with diamanté pins create a rich and romantic look. 'Grand Prix' and 'Black Baccara' roses are interspersed with red skimmia and *Viburnum tinus* berries, with trails of green ivy foliage.

# red is good with . . .

Red works well with all other colors except white, which makes red harsher, though lots of textural foliage can make this work. I like to use red with purple, burgundy, and blue, where it looks sophisticated. Lime green foliage, blossom, berries, and fillers take away some of the harshness of the red.

## . . . purple

BELOW A round hand-tied bouquet of 'Grand Prix' roses, burgundy ranunculus, and purple anemones mixed with skimmia is placed in a glass cylinder filled with cranberries.

## . . . primary colors

In this analogous color combination, deep red 'Grand Prix' roses and gloriosa lilies have been interspersed with pink and yellow gerberas, groups of orange leucospermums, and purple double eustoma.

## red is good with . . . cream

Creamy ornamental kale (*Brassica oleracea* 'Sunrise '99') is balanced against groups of 'Grand Prix' roses, *Hydrangea macrophylla* 'Rotshwarz', rose hips (*Rosa* 'Sensation'), and seeded eucalyptus.

# red is good with . . . yellow

Deep red 'Mango' calla lilies and hydrangea flowers contrast with green millet grass, yelllow achillea, 'Confetti' roses, salal, hypericum, and ivy.

# orange flowers

ORANGE IS A VIBRANT, WARM, and arresting color. It carries a lot less of the emotional baggage of red and is definitely seen as a fun color. The muddier, browner earthy tones of orange are the most fashionable. The lighter, brighter tones—the true color of citrus orange fruits—are used more in conjunction with other color schemes to produce a shocking and vibrant effect. We use fruit names to evoke bright tones—mango, peach, and apricot all describe orange shades—as well as metallic shades of copper, brass, and gold to also define this diverse and rich color.

1  2  3

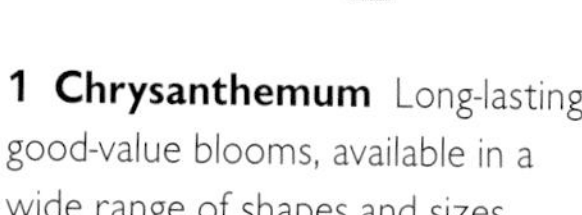

4 5 6 7

**1 Chrysanthemum** Long-lasting, good-value blooms, available in a wide range of shapes and sizes.

**2 Spurge** The long-stemmed branches of *Euphorbia fulgens* are useful accents in bouquets.

**3 Ranunculus** These look their best just before they expire, when their petals become translucent.

**4 Chinese lanterns** Physalis are popular for fall arrangements, particularly for Halloween.

**5 Bird of paradise** Resembling a beautiful bird, strelitzia is a wonderfully exotic flower.

**6 Calla lily** The funnel-shaped flowers look fantastic massed when you are feeling extravagant.

**7 Poppy** Suitable for massed and textural work, *Papaver* has cup-shaped flowers with papery petals.

OPPOSITE One of my favorite seasonal oranges comes in the form of the distinctive tall spires of *Kniphofia* (red hot poker).

## fall oranges

OPPOSITE Roses come in so many shades, and there are lots of wonderful orange varieties that look especially good in fall arrangements.

1 *Ilex aquifolium* 'Golden Verboon' (common holly) 2 *Solanum integrifolium* (tomato eggplant) 3 *Fagus sylvatica* (beech) 4 *Leucospermum cordifolium* 'Tango' (pincushion) 5 *Dendrobium* 'Tang' 6 *Ranunculus* 'Ranobelle Inra Oranjerood' 7 *Quercus robur* (English oak, common oak) 8 *Zantedeschia* 'Treasure' (arum lily, calla lily) 9 *Eucalyptus pulverulenta* 10 *Rosa* 'Macarena' 11 *Chrysanthemum* 'Reagan Orange' 12 *Euphorbia fulgens* 'Beatrix' 13 *Gladiolus* 'Esta Bonita' 14 *Chrysanthemum* 'Tom Pearce' 15 *Hippeastrum* 'Rilona' (amaryllis) 16 *Quercus palustris* (American oak) 17 *Tulipa* 'Prinses Irene'

I am drawn more to this color in the third quarter of the year. The warm mid range is the color of fall and the changing trees, the comforting color of an expectant harvest, and the plump produce of the pumpkin patch, full of promise for a fun Halloween.

# orange arrangements

ABOVE Giant-headed Clooney ranunculus are arranged in a low square dish, held in place in floral foam covered with green sand, and then edged with a tied frame of pussy willow.

LEFT This arrangement is built on a metal frame that holds four candles. 'High and Magic', 'Tucan', 'Marie-Claire', and 'Orange Juice' roses are mixed with dark ligustrum berries, *Leucospermum cordifolium* 'Succession', and the mini gerbera 'Wish', on a base of glossy camellia leaves.

OPPOSITE This textural table arrangement has roses and chrysanthemums mixed with orange celosia and seasonal apples. A mix of *Brachyglottis* 'Sunshine', *Alchemilla mollis*, skimmia, ivy berries, and photinia make it very natural.

OPPOSITE Pumpkins make long-lasting natural containers for floral arrangements. This one holds mini orange dahlias, rose hips, *Photinia* 'Red Robin', *Euphorbia fulgens* 'Sunstream', and *Viburnum tinus* berries, with a pillar candle wired in place through the center.

RIGHT A long and low fall centerpiece has heavy groups of dyed orange anemones, 'Tom Pearce' chrysanthemums, 'Orange Juice' and 'Eldorado' roses, *Echinacea purpurea* seed heads, and tied bunches of dried wheat. The base is a shallow dish filled with foam and covered with ivy berries.

ABOVE This loose, full autumnal arrangement is made up of cotoneaster berries, ivy berries, American oak, beech, skimmia, eucalyptus, Chinese lanterns, ornamental kales, and 'Léonidas' roses.

OPPOSITE This tall glass vase is filled with orange jalapeno peppers and topped with contorted willow with *Physalis alkekengi* 'Jumbo' and orange *Euphorbia fulgens* 'Sunstream'.

OPPOSITE A heavy metal urn has been decorated with thirty wired oranges and camellia leaves, placed into a cone of chicken wire filled with sphagnum moss.

RIGHT An enormous clear glass vase, filled with *Prunus* stems, is topped with a generously sized hand-tied bunch of orange 'Monarch Parrot' tulips. More of the *Prunus* stems, with buds just beginning to show on the bare wood, have been brought through to emerge from the very top of the arrangement to add height.

# orange is good with . . .

Orange mixes well with other colors. Mixed with lush green it is definitely tropical. With dark purple it is regal and in complete harmony. With a multicolored mix it becomes almost psychedelic. I also like wilder and more natural-looking autumnal arrangements with orange.

## . . . muted colors

ABOVE The brown, green, and sandy shades of these beans have been matched by the hand-tied posy of peonies, dahlias, fountain grass, hydrangea, *Alchemilla mollis*, and green dill.

## . . . contrasting colors

This vibrant mix includes 'Milva', 'Wow', and 'Milano' roses, 'Aisha' gerberas, *Leucospermum cordifolium* 'Tango', calendula, gloriosa, celosia, ivy berries, viburnum, camellia, and *Ruscus hypophyllum.*

## orange is good with . . . bright red

Leucospermums, elegant 'Mango' calla lilies, and orange 'Circus' roses blend with velvety 'Cherry Brandy' roses, 'Red Flair' hypericum, lotus seed heads, galax leaves, aspidistra, guelder roses, and white skimmia.

# yellow flowers

FOR ME THERE ARE TWO SEASONS for yellow flowers: the early spring when the seasonal daffodils and forsythia emerge and late summer when the achillea and sunflowers are in full bloom. In spring we relish the color after the bleakness of the winter and the short days. Recently, yellow has had a hard time as a flower color, and its wavering popularity is evident in the lack of varieties available. If a color is popular, the hybridizers very quickly spot the color trend and produce new flowers to supply the market. But yellow is undoubtedly a happy and warm color.

**1 Sunflower** Flowers with golden-yellow petals radiating from a large, distinctive dark center.

**2 Narcissus** Elegant spring flowers, in a range of yellow shades from creamy white to bright yellow.

**3 Cymbidium orchid** Extravagant but long-lasting cut flowers, these are good for weddings and event work.

**4 Ranunculus** Popular in bouquets and bridal work. Remove any lower foliage from the stems.

**5 Gerbera** Try to avoid touching the sensitive flower heads, which can be easily damaged.

**6 Calla lily** Versatile flowers, *Zantedeschia* are useful for all aspects of flower arranging.

**7 Rose** Still the most popular flower in the industry, due to its wide variation in color and size.

OPPOSITE The classic daffodil, that harbinger of spring, is great for vase arrangements and also in small posies and hand-tied bouquets.

## spring yellows

1 *Mimosa* 'Yellow Island' 2 *Pittosporum crassifolium* 'Variegatum' 3 *Helleborus argutifolius* 4 *Lysimachia clethroides* (white loosestrife) 5 *Genista tenera* 'Golden Shower' (broom) 6 *Tulipa* 'Weber's Parrot' 7 *Ranunculus* 'Ranobelle Donkergeel' 8 *Euphorbia fulgens* 'Quicksilver' 9 *Narcissus* 'Cheerfulness' 10 *Narcissus* 'Golden Ducat' 11 *Lathyrus odoratus* (sweet pea) 12 *Populus deltoides* (eastern cottonwood) 13 *Polianthes tuberosa* (tuberose) 14 *Euonymus fortunei* 'Emerald 'n' Gold' 15 *Tulipa* 'Monte Carlo' 16 *Zantedeschia* 'Florex Gold' (arum lily, calla lily) 17 *Rosa* 'Taxi' 18 *Spiraea nipponica* 'Snowmound' 19 *Antirrhinum majus* 'Winter Euro Yellow' (snapdragon) 20 *Gerbera germini* 'Kaliki' 21 *Viburnum opulus* (guelder rose) 22 *Abutilon vitifolium* var. *album* 23 *Eustoma grandiflorum* 'Piccolo Yellow' (lisianthus) 24 *Polygonatum* (solomon's seal) 25 *Forsythia* x *intermedia* 26 *Prunus glandulosa* 'Albo Plena'

## summer yellows

1 *Physalis alkekengi* (Chinese lantern) 2 *Populus deltoides* (eastern cottonwood) 3 *Crocosmia* 'Lucifer' (montbretia) 4 *Chrysanthemum* 'Salmon Fairie' 5 *Leucospermum reflexum* 'Lutea' (pincushion) 6 *Helenium* 'Moerheim Beauty' 7 *Zantedeschia* 'Florex Gold' (arum lily, calla lily) 8 *Capsicum annuum* 9 *Carthamus tinctorius* 'Kinko' (safflower, false saffron) 10 *Anethum graveolens* (dill) 11 *Hydrangea macrophylla* 12 *Rosa* 'Golden Gate' 13 *Helianthus annuus* 'Sonja' (sunflower) 14 *Hypericum* 'Jade Flair' (St. John's Wort) 15 *Chrysanthemum* 'Shamrock' 16 *Sandersonia aurantiaca* 17 *Malus* x *robusta* 'Red Sentinel' (crab apple)

Yellow is a popular corporate color, so I find that flowers in this bright primary color can work well in a variety of workplaces. Gold or yellow flowers are also traditionally requested to mark or decorate fiftieth—or golden—wedding anniversary celebrations.

# yellow arrangements

LEFT Grouping some flowers—sunflowers, Clooney ranunculus, rudbeckia, *Galax erceolata*, skimmia, broom, and mimosa—but using the length of others—calla lilies, flexigrass (*Xanthorrhoea australis*), and pussy willow—gives this arrangement movement and rhythm.

OPPOSITE A plastic bowl is covered in double-sided tape and encircled with yellow broom, into which two blocks of floral foam are added, with a chunky arrangement of cream 'Alexis' roses, 'Yellow Dot' roses, guelder roses, 'Daily Star' chrysanthemums, white skimmia, and some mixed sunflowers.

The sharp combination of *Hellebore argutifolius*, 'Dutch Master' daffodils, alder catkins, veronica, lysimachia, marguerite daisies, and yellow ranunculus, with its glowing yellows and acidic greens, is wonderfully refreshing.

Energy is suggested in this mass of plump buds and unfurling flowers. A posy of double peony tulips, scented *Mahonia aquifolium*, ranunculus, *Narcissus* 'Dick Wilden', and cream *Narcissus* 'Geranium' sits in a gray woven basket.

OPPOSITE This buffet table arrangement has been created by stacking three glass bowls on top of one another and then using rings of *Viburnum opulus*, *Alchemilla mollis*, green dill, and 'Mamma Mia' and 'Yellow Dot' roses.

RIGHT A ring of *Celosia* Cristata Group 'Bombay Yellow', sunflowers, crab apples, *Skimmia confusa* 'Kew Green', *Viburnum tinus* berries, *Alchemilla mollis*, ornamental kales (*Brassica oleracea* 'White Crane'), and 'Kaliki' mini gerberas surrounds a sheaf of yellow calla lilies (*Zantedeschia* 'Florex Gold') set in a pin holder and bound with a few stems of bear grass.

# yellow is good with . . .

I prefer to mix yellow with lots of green foliage or include it in a monochromatic color scheme, using a variety of yellows. Pale yellow works well with peach, orange, and also blue. To make yellow look more contemporary, I often use black vases. The contrast is sharp and arresting.

## . . . bright pinks

ABOVE Gloriosa lilies and *Rosa* 'Milano' contrast with yellow sunflowers, highlighted by *Viburnum opulus* 'Roseum', genista, *Asparagus umbellatus*, skimmia, camellia, and ivy.

## . . . peach and green

Cream 'Concordia' lilies, branches of forsythia, foxgloves, huge heads of hydrangea, coral peonies, and chrysanthemums make a strong impact and look appropriate in this sturdy verdigris urn.

# flowers around the home

OPPOSITE Everlasting sweet pea, feverfew, blackberry, valerian, wild teasels, Queen Anne's lace, sweet cicely, pink veronica, and musk mallow are each given their own recycled milk bottle vase, and the collection is bound together with gardener's twine.

**when I am arranging** flowers in my own home, I have my favorite spots. I always like to have something scented and usually place this in a large open space so it is not too overpowering. When it comes to vases, I have a huge collection, so I tend to pick the flowers first and then find a suitable container. I know from my clients that lots of people have a vase for a space, and then pick the flowers to go in that area. When I supply the flowers in someone else's house, I pick prominent spots—two or three well-placed vases are better than lots of little ones. If budgets are tight, I arrange single stems carefully to give the illusion of more flowers.

I prefer to use glass containers on my dining table, and usually only make my own containers when I am celebrating a special occasion or have friends for dinner. Ceramic vases tend to be my everyday home vases; I like to use jugs and old zinc florists' pots in my kitchen, where I prefer the flowers to look more casual. If I have house guests, then I love to arrange single stems on their bedside tables, and also always place a bowl of fragrant flowers in the bathrooms.

When buying flowers for my own home, I try to pick long-lasting flowers and make sure that at least one is seasonal. If I am saving my pennies, I use a vase of foliage or a collection of herbs so that I can use them later in my cooking. If I have a dinner party but funds are low, I might use a row of inexpensive plants on the table, which can work out much cheaper than a full-scale arrangement. Single-flower vases are also a great way of making a table look full on a budget. If you do not have any small vases, use votives or start saving decorative old glass jelly jars.

# glass

Glass is by far the most popular material for vases. It can add to the arrangement to be able to see the stems, and you can dress up and customize a glass container easily. There is a huge variety in sizes and shapes and it is good to have some from 7 inches to 15 inches for domestic-size bunches. Most flowers sold commercially are 20 to 30 inches long, so investing in tall, heavy-bottomed vases is worthwhile to create pleasing designs. On a practical note, when using glass, you can see how clean and high the water level is.

Individual gerbera stems in a variety of colors are suspended in water in a row of identical small glass cubes.

ABOVE This fishbowl arrangement was created for a charity competition among designers at the London flower market. It won first prize and has been one of my most imitated designs. 'Mango' calla lilies have been arranged with orange leucospermums in a bed of green Thai berries.

RIGHT These beautifully colored handmade glass vases by the artist Paul Williams have been diagonally spaced, starting with yellow ranunculus, deep blue hydrangea, lime green 'Shamrock' chrysanthemums, deep blue hyacinths, and pale yellow 'Winterberg' tulips.

LEFT This tall, thin vase arrangement is given actual physical and visual balance by the fritillarias and willow, and the collar of lilac hydrangea.

OPPOSITE Here, the trailing shape of the pink phalaenopsis orchids and dyed vine give movement to a contemporary arrangement in a simple clear glass vase.

To make this multicolored arrangement, insert a tumbler into a larger glass cube and line the gap with jelly beans. Top with a hand-tied bunch of roses, rose hips, *Viburnum tinus* berries, skimmia, hypericum, and *Alchemilla mollis*.

A manufactured glass bag vase from the German company Leonardo is filled with dainty pink *Vaccaria hispanica*. This shade of pink combines brilliantly with lime green for a fresh look.

ABOVE Fiery fall leaves are the color inspiration for this hand-tied bouquet of rose hips, skimmia, carthamus, beech, and roses, which has been placed into a vase within a fishbowl lined with chili peppers.

OPPOSITE A hand-tied bouquet of red peonies, red skimmia, lime green guelder roses, variegated carnations, and stems of flowering rhubarb has been arranged into rings of rhubarb in this early summer arrangement.

OPPOSITE A tricolored dogwood arrangement in green, red, and black has been used to line a block of foam within a glass cube vase. Three rows of roses—'Black Baccara', 'Jade', and 'Grand Prix'—have been arranged in straight lines to pick up the theme of the stripes of the dogwood.

RIGHT This small cylinder vase has been filled with swirls of thin-stemmed red Iranian dogwood, and a hand-tied posy of 'Grand Prix' roses edged with galax leaves has been placed on top.

LEFT Mixed Equadorian roses are arranged simply as a hand-tied posy and then placed in a smart black cube vase to highlight the fabulous variety of colors.

OPPOSITE Pink 'Barbie' and peach 'Prima Donna' roses have been mixed with photinia, *Viburnum opulus* 'Roseum', hyacinths, and celosia in a fun striped vase.

# ceramic

I often pick ceramic containers because of their bright colors. I adore stripes and spots and single colors, but rarely feel attracted to any that are too decorative or floral. Sometimes I even take my inspiration for a design from the container itself. They are versatile and cheap, and smaller ones created to serve as plant pot covers are also the right height to make into table centers. Aged, antique, and worn pots also work well with flowers, as they tend to look more natural. Black or deep brown looks smart and works well for contemporary designs.

A hand-tied bunch of white *Tulipa* 'Honeymoon' and pink *Tulipa* 'Bell Song', with a collar of entwined pussy willow, makes a simple spring display in a rustic ribbed vase.

I have quite a collection of these oil pots from Provence, and this is one of my largest. It is filled with foxgloves and coral and red peonies, mixed with dark purple *Prunus* and the dangly explosions of fountain grass.

OPPOSITE Ultrafeminine and ultrapretty: a domed hand-tied bouquet of 'Rosita Vendela' roses sits in a pot that has been spray painted shocking pink to match.

ABOVE In this low square container a structure of kiwi vine has been created, providing a frame through which flexigrass has been woven. 'Cognac' anthuriums have been added for a light, well-balanced arrangement.

LEFT The varied colors of 'Sphinx', 'Wow', 'Grand Prix', and 'Sunbeam' roses, *Viburnum opulus* 'Roseum', *Hyacinthus orientalis* 'Blue Star', *Anemone coronaria*, *Hydrangea* 'Challenge Blue', *Chrysanthemum* 'Shamrock', *Ranunculus* 'Ranobelle Inra Wit', coral fern (*Gleichenia polypodiodes*), ivy, and *Hypericum inodorum* 'King Flair' were suggested by the palette shown in the stripes on the vase.

The dark dahlias and black centers of the germini gerberas make these vibrant late-summer bunches coordinate perfectly with the repeated dark cube vases.

The soft tones of this pale pink Provençal cooking bowl inspired this arrangement of *Cosmos* 'Black Beauty', carnations, ligularia leaves, blackberries, and 'Sweet Avalanche+' roses.

This charming oversize pink and white spotted teacup immediately made me think of cream 'Talea+' and pink 'Belle Rose' roses, whose coloring perfectly reflects the container.

LEFT Eggplants were cut in half and scored to clip on the sides of a straight-sided plastic bowl for a natural basket. Moss fills in the gaps and the vegetables have been secured with raffia.

OPPOSITE Woven strips of variegated New Zealand flax, versatile and long-lasting, line a glass cube of pink 'Telstar' amaryllis.

# natural materials

I love to make my own containers so that the design takes on a more sculptural effect. For the base, I use plastic or glass and double-sided tape to fix the plant material to the container. If the plant material is heavier, such as fruit or vegetables, I prefer to use a sturdy basket. The least expensive plant material is local leaves, so I use laurel and rhododendron leaves from the garden, or I buy long-lasting aspidistra leaves. Later in the year, I like to use vegetables as containers—I used watermelons at a rustic wedding and pumpkins at a harvest supper.

OPPOSITE A chicken-wire basket, externally lined with lengths of rosemary and blossom, is filled with roses, ranunculus, lilac, and *Viburnum opulus* 'Roseum'.

ABOVE A single 'Tom Pearce' chrysanthemum is encircled by *Rosa* 'Amazing Fantasy', *Salix babylonica* var. *pekinensis* 'Tortuosa', and *Quercus palustris*. Autumnal leaves fixed with double-sided tape and tied with sisal cover the glasses.

BELOW Globe artichokes were cut in half, then wired to fix them around a block of foam to form a vegetative basket, which holds 'Circus' roses, dahlias, peonies, green dill, *Viburnum opulus* berries, and hebe.

OPPOSITE To create this glaucous green container, core out the center of a Savoy cabbage and fit a polystyrene cup filled with floral foam in it to hold 'Milano', 'Wow', and 'Grand Prix' roses, and skimmia.

OPPOSITE This still-life design uses flowers, branches, leaves, and berries to create a rust-colored landscape of trees, bushes, and ground cover. The base is created from a block of foam covered with cinnamon sticks cut to the same length and glued in place. *Celastrus orbiculatus* (Oriental bittersweet), beech leaves, *Gerbera jamesonii* 'Baynard', *Rosa* 'Léonidas', *Cotinus coggygria* f. *purpurea*, dill, and fruiting ivy are used in the display.

ABOVE To create this fresh lime green basket, use heavy- gauge stub wires to wire the apples, then attach the fruits to the outer edge of a sturdy basket.

LEFT Colored Mikado sticks were fixed to a glass cube covered with double-sided tape, then 'Happy' roses were pushed into floral foam inside the cube.

OPPOSITE A selection of cottage garden flowers, including valerian, foxgloves, honeysuckle, and lupins, is placed in a pair of bright pink rubber boots.

# unusual containers

I am always on the lookout for unconventional containers for my flower designs, and love to create whimsical or quirky designs in handbags, boxes, even children's boots. Some of the inspiration for this comes from the items themselves, and some from working over the years for clients that yearn for something different. We have used live fish in bowls for corporate clients, birdcages, and teapots on tables for weddings; junkyard bottles, lamp shades, hats, and even shoes for parties. For a Bar Mitzvah we once even used footballs!

PANTONE®
239 C

OPPOSITE The perfect desk accessory—*Dianthus* 'Farida' with *Alchemilla mollis*, 'Leila' germini gerberas, and *Origanum* 'Gijsie' in an iconic Pantone pink mug.

RIGHT When I spotted these ceramic pink waffle-cone vases in a shop, I thought they would be perfect for a floral take on the quintessentially English ice cream known as a "99," which consists of a chocolate flake placed into an ice-cream cone. Here the appropriately named pink 'Barbie' and green 'Peppermint' roses have been arranged in foam to look like dollops of ice cream on a cone.

OPPOSITE A hand-tied posy of 'Barcelona' tulips, aqua packed in cellophane, sits in a sequinned bag. We make lots of these for bridesmaids' posies, as they are easy to carry. Pink roses would work as well.

RIGHT A deep pink bamboo basket is filled with *Chenopodium quinoa* 'Carina', *Nigella* 'Pink Power', *Alchemilla mollis*, cotinus, and *Asclepias* 'Amalia'.

BELOW Little buckets decorated with licorice candies have been filled with posies of pink carnations, roses, cabbages, lemon germini gerberas, red daisy chrysanthemums, blue eryngium, and eucalyptus.

OPPOSITE Single heads of bright pink ranunculus are arranged in small water-holding vials in delicate banana skin bags, allowing the innate beauty of the flower to be highlighted.

# repeat designs

There is a vogue for repeating an arrangement by placing a collection of identical designs together. At its most undemanding, this might be positioning bottles or vases together, each holding just one flower. It may have an asymmetrical theme or it may be a mass of one type of flower repeated many times. Repetition gives movement and it makes a stronger visual impact. Thirty small bubble vases with one daisy in each are more arresting than thirty stems of daisies in one vase.

I love to use small pots of flowers down a long table—it gives you a chance to use delicate, small flowers, such as fritillaria, *Muscari*, and lily of the valley. As a finishing touch, I tied ivy leaves around the pots with raffia.

OPPOSITE Floral foam balls in different sizes have been massed with the daisy-like heads of the green-centered chrysanthemum 'Dark Rosy Reagan'.

RIGHT Three red, glass tear vases have been topped with round floral-foam balls decorated with germini gerberas. These chunky arrangements are made visually more attractive by the design being repeated.

LEFT Two very simple vase arrangements are grouped together for more visual impact. Each vase has a bunch of Iranian dogwood, one cymbidium orchid, and one *Monstera* leaf.

OPPOSITE Tightly packed hand-tied bunches of *Alchemilla mollis*, tulips, hyacinths, and hydrangeas are repeateted in pink fishbowl vases along a table.

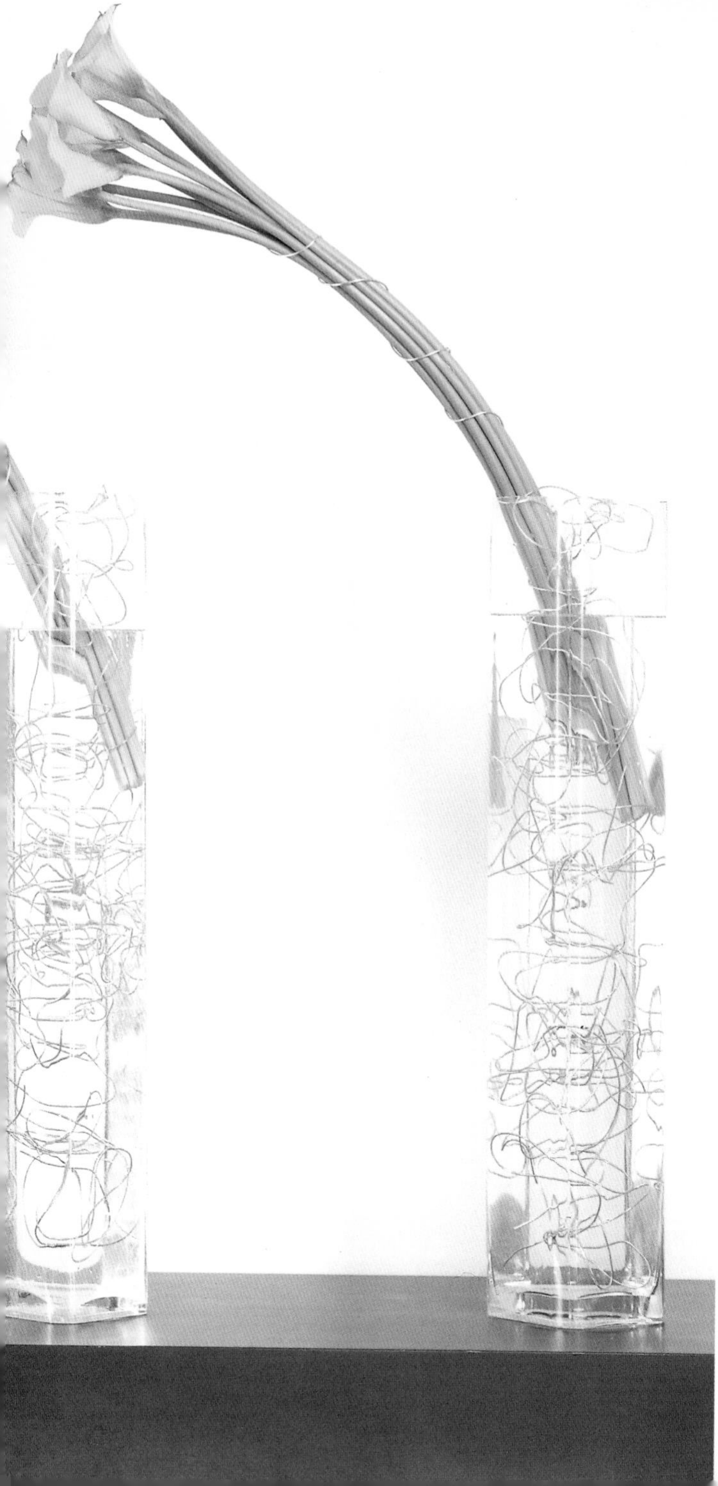

LEFT Asymmetrical arrangements grouped together remain very popular. The long-stemmed calla lilies have been bunched with swirls of wire to keep the flower heads in place. The effect makes a strong impact.

BELOW Three vases have been filled with anthurium heads suspended by gold aluminum wire. It is best to build this up from the bottom of the vase to the top, then fill it with water to keep the flowers from floating to the top.

LEFT Palm tree bark was glued onto a straw and wire frame to make this wreath. The *Dendrobium* orchid heads were hot glued on top to create a contrast of color and texture.

OPPOSITE A mossed wreath was based with ivy berries and red skimmia, then groups of roses, gloriosa lilies, gerberas, baby eggplants, limes, and yellow peppers were individually wired to the frame.

# wreaths

Traditionally wreaths were made to commemorate an occasion or the passing of a friend or relative. Door rings used to be confined to the winter months when our gardens are less productive, but in this section we have taken the all-year-round approach. It is lovely to have a welcoming seasonal ring on your door, especially when you have a celebration in the house. Most wreaths have a base of sphagnum moss into which we pin plant material. Dried plant material can be glued or wired onto vines or a circle of twigs. Straw and styrofoam can also be used as a base, and the only limit to your design is your imagination.

OPPOSITE This sculptural wreath relies on shades of green and fantastic textures for its effect. I have used *Muscari*, hyacinths, and small-leaved succulent plants (*Pachyphytum*) in miniature terra-cotta pots, some *Tillandsia* leaves, and sphagnum and bun moss wired to a wreath frame.

RIGHT A mossed wreath frame was decorated with hummocks of bun moss, hazel twigs, ranunculus, and calla lilies. Some white plastic eggs and real quail eggs have been glued directly onto the wreath using a hot-glue gun.

LEFT You don't have to rely on flowers for glorious color and texture. A mixture of fresh apples, clementines, limes, and lemons, and dried limes, orange slices, and apple slices, and whole nuts were wired in groups on a frame covered in sphagnum moss.

OPPOSITE Hung on your front door, this glorious summer wreath, packed with roses, peony tulips, sweet peas, white phlox, eustoma, hebe, pistachio berries, *Alchemilla mollis*, and galax leaves, would be a fantastic welcome for your guests.

OPPOSITE There is a strong sense of movement to this wreath, with the green stems and leaves of 'White Dream' tulips and 'Black Eyed Beauty' calla lilies swirling among the dark *Prunus* stems.

LEFT For this bark and crab apple wreath, lengths of silver birch bark were glued to a large floral-foam wreath. The crab apples were wired to the foam. Fruits are all best wired, as they are heavy and fleshy. They are kept in place by the moss tucked in as filler.

RIGHT If you are planning to glue a lot of small items, such as star anise, you could invest in a glue pan. This allows you to use a brush to paint on the hot glue, and then you can stick the dried items to the dry foam base more quickly.

LEFT This wonderfully textural fall wreath, set on a base of a mossed ring, has an abundant seasonal mix of *Viburnum opulus* berries, apples, chestnuts, some very realistic fake mushrooms, lotus seed heads, alder catkins, and berries from *Solanum integrifolium*.

OPPOSITE This natural scented wreath has a Christmas feel. A swirling frame of birch covers a base of pine. Colorful satin ribbon was woven through the foliage, then groups of glittery pears, fir cones, and dried lotus seed heads were added. Heavily wired dried oranges and lengths of cinnamon add to the sensual fragrance.

# flowers for giving

OPPOSITE A hand-tied bouquet containing a wonderful selection of favorite flowers, such as roses, dahlias, tulips, peonies, and hyacinths, is a gift that will always be greatly received.

**giving flowers is one** of life's great pleasures. Whenever I am planning a gift bouquet, I think first of the recipient. So if I do not know them, I try to get some information about them that will inform my choice of flowers. When a variety of flower or a color has been decided, then I think about a good combination. Ideally one might also think about some fragrance, some texture, and also give some thought to the longevity of the flowers. A hand-tied bouquet, which is perfect for presenting as a gift, is created by taking a bunch of flowers and foliage and spiraling them in the hand to create a perfect bunch for a vase. Usually, in a mixed bouquet, foliage will be about a third of the plant material, and ideally I like to use three different types to make the bouquet look and feel natural. In the fall and winter, this may include berries or rose hips; in the spring and summer, it is more likely to include blossom or flowering greenery and grasses. The average-size bouquet will have around twenty-five to thirty-five stems, including flowers and foliage, for a reasonably full effect.

If you want to create a lavish bouquet for a special occasion, you could use stems of cymbidium orchids, long-stemmed roses, and lilies that command high stem prices. For a cheaper bouquet, you might think about more seasonal flowers or using all-year-round plant material, both of which are less expensive options. Shorter flowers are always less expensive than longer ones, and most bouquets are around 16 inches in length, so it is an important consideration to buy or select shorter flower varieties if you do not want to end up with a grand bouquet. If you want to make a huge gesture, then it is worth investing in flowers in the 32- to 40-inch-length range.

PAULA PRYK

The starting point of so many of the bouquets we are asked to make as gifts is a bunch of beautiful roses.

# bouquets

Different styles of bouquets can be created, depending on the type of flowers and the recipients. Small, delicate flowers look best spiraled into posies. Most round shapes and fillers work well in round bouquets, but some shapes, particularly spires or raceme-style flowers, which carry a number of flowers on a stem, such as delphinium, *Eremurus*, cymbidium orchids, or aconitum, are best displayed in long bouquets. The technique is the same in that you arrange the flowers in your hand, but the choice of material will make the bouquet more structured.

ABOVE The Victorian posy—where massed flowers are placed in concentric circles—is a classic design. This one was hand tied by working circles around a central rose. Widow iris, blue *Muscari*, and white narcissus follow, then it is edged with violets.

RIGHT This delightful posy is a modern take on an old idea, with its structural ring of fresh contorted willow surrounding *Fritillaria meleagris*, 'Winterberg' tulips, *Narcissus tazetta* 'Avalanche', *Muscari botryoides* 'Album', and a central 'Alexis' rose.

An early summer hand-tied bouquet mixes lilac, guelder roses, anemones, and ranunculus with red summer peonies.

This scented spring posy of lilac, guelder roses, daffodils, mimosa, freesia, ranunculus, and tulips ('Negrita' and 'Madison Garden') is a packed bundle of delight.

LEFT A popular color combination for bouquets intended as gifts is pink, lilac, and lime green. This spiraled hand-tied bouquet of pink astilbe, cerise 'Milano' roses, dahlias, peonies, hydrangea, and double purple eustoma is made more vibrant by using the lime green foliages of fountain grass and *Viburnum opulus*. The spiky 'Green Revert' chrysanthemum has a slightly less acidic tone than the shamrock chrysanthemum often used.

OPPOSITE Trails of jasmine and a decadent pink feather trim that echoes the airy feel of the astilbe and *Alchemilla mollis* augment a grouped bouquet of 'Barbie' roses, campanula, and hydrangea flowers.

LEFT A tropical bouquet of cymbidium orchids, snake grass, leucospermum, *Euphorbia fulgens*, aspidistra leaves, *Liriope gigantea*, and willow is tied with textured paper and orange raffia.

OPPOSITE This beautiful cream and green bouquet was aqua packed in clear cellophane, and then swathed in cream deconet.

# wrapping

I especially like to use natural wrappings, such as by-products of the coconut or banana family. Sometimes we use fresh leaves to wrap a bouquet, such as banana leaves that are sold in the fruit market for Thai restaurants and Asian cuisine, or aspidistra leaves. We also use a variety of man-made fibers and papers for wrapping, from soft Japanese paper and firm netting to feathers and silk organza, as well as printed and frosted cellophane. Each collection of flowers gets a different wrapping according to flower type, purpose, and budget.

Hand-tied mixed dahlias have been generously cocooned with matching pink fabric wrap and ribbon.

Wrappings can be natural—peonies, phlox, sweet peas, *Alchemilla mollis*, hebe, and rosemary are surrounded by a collar formed from cut sections of banana leaves.

Black fabric is an unusual choice, but it makes the perfect wrapping to set off the colors of this deep-toned, autumnal-themed bouquet.

Orange fabric echoes the fiery tones of the red American oak, red eucalyptus, red skimmia, 'Mango' calla lilies, echinacea, and sunflowers, with sharp highlights of 'Green Shamrock' chrysanthemums and green dill.

OPPOSITE This cheerful mix includes roses, rose hips, flowering eucalyptus, larch, orange dill, cream and green ornamental kales, and spiky standard chrysanthemums.

RIGHT Color is the theme of this hand-tied bouquet, with orange predominating the selection of ivy berries, *Brachyglottis*, *Sandersonia*, *Papaver*, 'Apricot Parrot' tulips, mimosa, *Myrica gale* myrtle foliage, *Rosa* 'Fiesta+', and the guelder rose.

LEFT Two-toned 'Fiesta+', 'Two Faces+', and cream 'Lemonade' roses, and cestrum, *Ozothamnus diosmifolius* 'Champion Pink', Oriental poppies, and kangaroo paw are aqua packed and wrapped with soft peach fabric.

OPPOSITE Bright color combinations need to be blended together by the addition of dark green glossy leaves, such as rhododendron, and also here the burgundy *Photinia* 'Red Robin' leaves.

# valentine's day

Red roses continue to be the popular choice on this occasion. Global demand for this flower is so huge that it causes supply problems and the price is forced sky-high. My own alternative choices for bouquets at this time of year are tulips or ranunculus, both of which are in season in February. I also think orchids are a good choice; they have romantic connotations and they last so well. They are usually expensive, but when you consider the price of roses at this time, they offer good value.

Large-headed Clooney ranunculus are mixed with black 'Queen of the Night' tulips, 'Extase' and 'Grand Prix' roses, plus a few peonies. Trails of ivy placed across the tall, red martini-style glass vase give rhythm to the arrangement.

I like to edge hand-tied designs with folded aspidistra leaves, which are inexpensive and make a very fetching valentine bouquet. One round of leaves accentuates the massed 'Coolwater', 'Milano', and 'Ruby Red' roses within.

OPPOSITE A large, open floral-foam heart frame was edged with ivy trails wired to the base and then topped with a mass of multicolored roses. More ivy tails and *Muehlenbeckia* vines give a natural feel, while faux butterflies complete the design.

RIGHT This polished copper heart was made for me by a group of talented German florists trading as Belle Art. Extravagantly filled with long gloriosa lilies and garlanded with short gloriosa, this would woo anyone in the floral trade!

Roses remain the first choice for many romantics, and in this bouquet, they are given a contemporary twist with a collar of red Iranian dogwood.

A large hand-tied posy of cream and pink 'Anna' roses—the perfect alternative to the more usual red for a Valentine's bouquet.

LEFT Ten stems of the pale pink rose 'Universe' have been hand tied, aqua packed, and placed into a small sequinned basket for a very feminine arrangement.

OPPOSITE Anemones, *Muscari*, *Viburnum opulus*, 'Blue Diamond' tulips, 'Blue Pacific' roses, 'Weber's Parrot' tulips, 'Atlantic' hyacinths, cream ranunculus, and a touch of birch catkins have been spiraled into a hand-tied bouquet trimmed with netting.

# mother's day

This is one of my favorite days in the retail calendar, as you get to meet lots of young customers who are instinctively drawn to flowers. They often pick some challenging combinations for bouquets for their moms, but it is always a lot of fun. It is the single most important day on the florist's calendar and the busiest worldwide. Spring is such a wonderful time for flowers that there are so many options in either March, which is when Mothering Sunday falls in the United Kingdom, or in May, which is when the rest of the world celebrates Mother's Day.

This delightful hand-tied bouquet of *Cytisus*, *Viburnum opulus*, 'Jan Bos' hyacinths, and 'Blenda' tulips, all swathed in pink tissue, will definitely make someone's Mother's Day!

These spring flowers have lots of fleshy, soft stems, so instead of using floral foam, I have chosen to use a bowl containing water and chicken wire, which will be easier to use and will help the longevity of the flowers.

OPPOSITE This oversize glass teacup has a slightly *Alice in Wonderland* feel and is a fun touch for a Mother's Day present. It is filled with petals and mixed roses.

ABOVE A simple glass bowl was filled with fake crystals threaded on thin aluminum wire and five pink 'Tuscani' roses.

LEFT Diagonal lines of pink 'Dolce Vita', 'Aqua', 'Milano', 'Pink Renate', and 'Poison' roses are arranged in foam covered by pink grit and edged with *Equisetum*.

OPPOSITE A birthday cake arrangement is designed on a "posy pad" of foam covered with camellia, asparagus fern, astrantia, *Asclepias* 'Moby Dick', and 'Cherry Brandy' roses.

# birthdays

When it comes to presenting flowers as a gift to someone on their birthday, it is always nice to send something you have put together especially for them. Sometimes I enjoy the challenge of arranging a bouquet from my own garden for a friend. If I am buying flowers, I usually consider what kind of flowers I feel represent the person, the colors they might like, and then see if I can add scent and seasonal flowers. Men often respond to bright or primary colors and interesting textures, whereas women prefer paler hues and are keener on fragrance.

For this arrangement, a low bowl was placed inside another bowl to create a gap in which to display a selection of multicolored jelly beans. The central container is filled with foam and arranged with *Viburnum opulus*, ivy berries, and mixed Clooney ranunculus to match the tapered candles.

Here the bowl is filled with pot pourri, and its colors are matched by dark red peonies, pink, brown, and lilac roses, yellow achillea, *Tanacetum*, purple sweet peas, variegated weigela, and *Alchemilla mollis*.

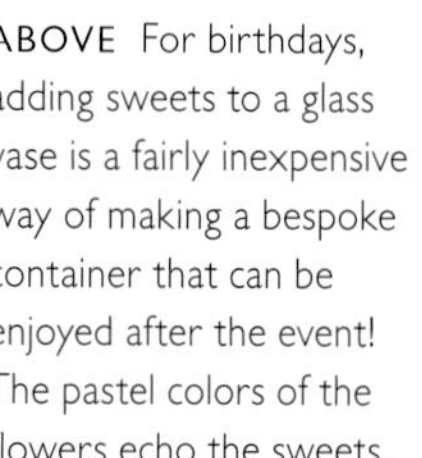

ABOVE For birthdays, adding sweets to a glass vase is a fairly inexpensive way of making a bespoke container that can be enjoyed after the event! The pastel colors of the flowers echo the sweets.

RIGHT A stationery box was filled with roses to match the stripes: 'Milano', 'Mamma Mia', 'Black Baccara', 'Cool Water', 'Barbie', and white 'Bianca' dyed blue, mixed with *Skimmia japonica*.

# decorating your table

OPPOSITE Bar and buffet tables are great for tall arrangements that act as focal points. Here, a tall-stemmed vase has been filled with a huge hand-tied bouquet that has been filled with plump, rich purple berries, to add further color and visual interest.

**the practice of adorning tables** with flowers, herbs, and petals dates as far back as ancient Greece and Rome and has endured to the present day. Flower arranging is an art form that enhances the quality of life, and anyone who loves flowers wants to be able to arrange them more effectively and creatively. Once this was just the preserve of the rich, but nowadays the purchase of a bunch of flowers has very much become part of the weekly shop. The growth of the flower industry and the widespread road and airfreight of this once-fragile commodity means that inexpensive flowers are now available to everyone throughout the year.

As most celebrations include food and drink, it is inevitable that your table will be the focus, so your floral centerpieces are of paramount importance—flowers bring luxury, beauty, and fragrance. Floral arrangements can be of differing heights, depending on the size and style of your venue, and can be in an infinite variety of containers. As well as the flowers, other ways of dressing your table include the use of linens and candles. I like to use white and ivory linen for white flowers, and also when the flowers are multicolored, as the neutral background gives a better effect. You can use a few small details to personalize your table, and they can be simple to construct. Candles and votives are an inexpensive way of making an impact as well as creating great ambient lighting. My favorite way to decorate my own table is to use seasonal fruits and vegetables in my table designs, and this can often be an economical way of making more of a display, too. I also love to use vines or trails down the center of a table, and then arrange small tumblers filled with posies to complement them.

RIGHT The colors of a striped runner have been copied in the flowers on a long floral-foam rack. The flowers include hydrangea, 'Cool Water', 'Peppermint', 'Amalia', 'Wow', and 'Marie-Claire' roses, cotinus, green sedum, ivy foliage, echinops, red dahlias, yellow achillea, green hydrangea, and blue scabious.

# centerpieces

Usually we create round arrangements for round tables and long arrangements for rectangular tables. Round tables are difficult to talk across, particularly large ones, so we often we use taller arrangements on those so the guests can look under the arrangement but they still have a great impact in the room. Long tables give you the opportunity to make lovely linear horizontal designs. In my own home, I prefer to make lots of smaller arrangements and dot them along a rectangular table, because I like to reserve space for food platters and serving bowls.

LEFT Scented stocks, massed together with a collar of twisted allium stems, demonstrate their full palette of pinks through to purple. Although you can buy stocks all year round, they are less expensive in their natural season.

OPPOSITE Branching stems of pink phalaenopsis orchids have been hand tied and placed into a long, clear glass cylinder vase filled with pink aluminum wire and suspended orchids.

**tall** Large flat rings can be given more height by using a bowl and pin holder in the center, from which you can arrange some taller central flowers. Visually, using one type of flower can make tall arrangements look more impressive, and this can also be more cost effective.

OPPOSITE Pin holders are very useful for anchoring a few flowers into a low container or the center of a ring. They are used mostly for minimal flower designs or for Japanese Ikebana. I tend to use them for tall architectural flowers, such as these *Allium* 'Purple Sensation'.

RIGHT 'Pink Panther' and 'Karl Rosenfield' peonies are interspersed with *Alchemilla mollis* and trails of asparagus fern. To add further texture and color, the clear glass vase has been layered with cherries and faux summer berries, alternated with cut clear cellophane.

LEFT The base of this cone-shaped topiary is soaked green floral foam covered with chicken wire wired into a verdigris urn. Try to choose large-headed flowers so they cover the shape fairly quickly—if you use small-headed flowers, you may be surprised to find just how long a design like this may take to produce! I chose hydrangea, peonies, and 'Vendella' and 'Popov' roses, and filled in with soft fragrant flowers, including sweet peas, philadelphus, and phlox.

OPPOSITE This classic wedding topiary uses skimmia and ivy berries as the base with 'Vendella', 'Illusion', and 'Old Dutch' roses and hydrangea. Trails of scented stephanotis are used to soften the shape.

**low** The compact arrangement is our most frequently requested shape and style because it can be modified to all budgets and occasions. It is easy to create, works in any venue, and can be made to any size. Smaller versions of table centerpieces can be produced for side tables and coffee tables.

LEFT A green-leafed bowl is filled with a rounded display of *Viburnum opulus*, hydrangea, blackberries, and 'Grand Prix', 'Milano', and 'Milva' roses.

OPPOSITE The colors of a central table runner have been mirrored in the flower designs and tableware. Three square dishes contain brightly colored roses and kumquats. Deep red vanda orchids are dotted along the *Muehlenbeckia* vine.

Fresh lavender has been bunched into a swag with wired fennel bulbs to create a lovely natural garden feel. Green and white hydrangea and blowsy garden roses are grouped on a base of *Viburnum tinus* berries.

I have always loved to use leeks in my arrangements, because I love the graduation of color from the the roots to the lush green stems. Baby leeks were placed around a small glass cylinder, and then filled with a hand-tied bouquet of *Viburnum opulus*, *Alchemilla mollis*, white peonies, and 'Renate' roses.

Small lengths of Japanese knotweed have been used to edge a Perspex tray of 'Avalanche+', pink 'Sweet Avalanche+', and 'Peach Avalanche+' roses.

ABOVE This low boat-shaped container is very useful, and I use it often for table arrangements; here it is filled with assorted roses and rosebuds, astrantia, *Brachyglottis* 'Sunshine', and *Viburnum opulus*.

RIGHT For a summer arrangement, this grouping of hydrangea, *Alchemilla mollis*, astrantia, cotinus, blackberries, and garden roses, with individual terra-cotta pots wired into it, gives a charming cottage garden feel.

Blowsy 'Shirley Temple' peonies have been mixed with silver eryngium, *Rosa* 'Two Faces+', dark burgundy *Cotinus coggygria* 'Royal Purple', silver *Brachyglottis* 'Sunshine', 'Phillipa' garden roses, and sweet peas. The swirling shapes of the petals reflect the movement in the design of the tablecloth.

LEFT For a summer lunch table, the graphic design on the place mats has been copied in the flower arrangements by using a random color combination of individual heads of scabious, sunflower, 'Grand Prix' rose, marguerite daisy, pink and white 'Cézanne' rose, and a yellow and orange 'Circus' rose. Turquoise aluminum wire keeps the flowers in place.

OPPOSITE A vibrant selection of late-summer flowers, including dahlias, achillea, zinnias, and scabious, is mixed with dill and *Alchemilla mollis*. Individual zinnias have been laid on the napkins. All of the elements—the runner, the vases, the napkins, and the glassware—are brought together by the colors.

**repeated designs** When you are creating a number of arrangements in one room, you notice how the multiplication of the design makes the impact greater. When you place one on each table, the visual effect is diluted, but if you place two or more together, then their effect is increased.

OPPOSITE A series of single vases displays the eccentric-looking *Allium* 'Schubertii'. The metallic tones of the flower set off the stainless-steel table in a very cool-feeling setting.

ABOVE These black- and-white arrangements consist of dahlias, with cotinus and *Daucas carota* 'Dara'. A single white phalaenopsis orchid placed on each black napkin gives a sophisticated feel to the table.

OPPOSITE Repeated glass cubes in green and dark blue hold identical selections of vibrantly colored gloriosa lilies, poppies, *Viburnum opulus*, fruiting ivy, ranunculus, and hyacinths.

RIGHT Monochromatic displays are simple to construct and can be very effective when used more than once. I love the hot colors of zinnias and used them here with coordinating grit. Faux butterflies add the finishing touch.

ABOVE Hand-tied bouquets of 'Classic Duett', 'Dance Ballet', 'Renate', and 'Toucan' roses are set in low bowls filled with crab apples. Autumnal leaves line red votives, and mulberry twigs with wild clematis and crab apples garland the table.

OPPOSITE The patterns and colors of a pretty paper tablecloth and accessories have been brought to life by these cube vases filled with roses, zinnias, and *Alchemilla mollis* for a summer barbecue.

LEFT Glass votives filled with pink gypsophila, white ranunculus, *Muscari*, and sprigs of white lilac are placed on a wirework candelabra. A garland for the table was created by wiring bunches of flowers to asparagus ferns.

OPPOSITE This mossed candelabra was decorated with *Acacia*, *Stephanandra incisa* 'Crispa', Portugal laurel, roses, astilbe, hydrangea, and hypericum. Dried bunches of lavender have also been used as extra decoration at the foot of the candelabra.

# candelabras

Branched candleholders might be one of the oldest decorations for a table, and while they may have lost their essential utilitarian role, they are still the most often used. They are extremely versatile and can be dressed up to suit the venue and the theme of almost any event.

LEFT Rose petals sprinkled across the table and at the base of the long taper candles echo the roses used in the ring circling the base of this crystal candelabra.

OPPOSITE Floral-foam wreath rings holding *Pieris japonica*, 'Timeless' roses, camellia, 'Gipsy Queen' hyacinths, ranunculus, and a touch of *Alchemilla mollis* surround repeated green glass candelabra.

OPPOSITE This candelabra has been decorated with ruscus, eucalyptus, and variegated ivy, with *Alchemilla mollis* and a selection of garden roses for a predominantly pastel-toned color theme.

RIGHT The base of this candelabra was covered with wet floral foam and moss. A wreath frame was placed on the branches of the candelabra so that lots of flowers could be added to the top. Wired into this framework are birch twigs with catkins, spring jasmine, ivy, lilac blossoms, purple eustoma, and groups of 'Blue Pacific' roses.

LEFT I love making candelabras into living topiary shapes by adding greenery or flowers for special events. Rosemary, ivy, and box are some of my favorite foliage to use at any time of the year, but in the spring, blossom or flowering stems of all types look great wound around the structure.

OPPOSITE It is a nice idea to place decorations at table level to complement the height of a candelabra. This metal one has been covered with pink flowering *Prunus* and sprigs of pink gypsophila to echo the pink candles. A ring of ivy berries, 'Sweet Akito' roses, pale pink ranunculus, and pink gypsophila encircles the base.

LEFT A rich red 'Black Baccara' rose is surrounded by hypericum and ivy berries and tied with fresh lime green ribbon.

OPPOSITE Three yellow ranunculus (my favorite flower) have been tied with raffia for a simple but striking napkin decoration.

# napkin decorations

Floral napkin ties can add a lavish touch to a large formal celebration or a rather personal simple touch to a dinner party. They are an easy way to make a statement and personalize a table. For formal events, we often trim a napkin with ribbon and create a bed for the flowers, or use a sprig of herbs to decorate the napkin and scent the table. Posies placed on each napkin rather than creating single or even several table centerpieces can be a personal way of decorating the table and are a lovely way to make a few flowers appear very special to your guests.

A gloriosa lily is tied with a pink mousseline bow to a napkin. The inscription on the ribbon reads "The flower is a leaf mad with love" by the German philosopher Goethe.

A rose ('Xtreme') mixed with elderberries, ivy berries, skimmia, and American oak leaf has been arranged in a water vial covered with an aspidistra leaf and tied with sea grass, as a fresh floral favor.

**OPPOSITE** Napkin decorations can be very simple. The contrast of a pure white phalaenopsis orchid head placed on a black napkin is starkly graphic and gives a very sophisticated feel to a place setting.

**RIGHT** A single head of 'Ice Queen' gerbera tops the crisply starched and pyramid-folded napkin.

OPPOSITE Ivy, *Viburnum tinus*, and *Helleborus orientalis*, with subtle green shading, are held in a water vial covered with a laurel leaf and tied with raffia.

RIGHT Napkin flowers are a lovely way of bringing the color of other flowers across the table. Here, forget-me-nots, hellebores, and spring blossom make a very pretty spring touch.

OPPOSITE For me, this yellow-themed posy is the very essence of spring: *Prunus* blossom, mimosa, and primroses are tied with a green ribbon.

BELOW Woody stemmed herbs, such as these intertwined stems of thyme and rosemary, make perfect culinary-themed rings.

ABOVE What could be simpler, and yet more elegant? Two cymbidium orchid heads are wired together and attached to bear grass wrapped around a flat, folded napkin.

# special events

**OPPOSITE** Grouped gloriosa, bright pink 'Milano' roses, 'Kansas' peonies, orange 'Colandro' roses, orange 'Tango' leucospermums, 'Lill Orange' zinnias, and yellow *Achillea* 'Moonshine' with *Viburnum opulus* berries and *Corylus maxima* 'Red Filbert' circle floating candles.

**after many years in the** flower business, I still get a real buzz from decorating a special event, either for a client, a dear friend, or in my own home for friends and family. Making the table look lovely, creating a table design with some beautiful flowers, and sharing food and wine with friends is one of life's great pleasures. It does not have to be extravagant or take lots of time. Often it is in the little details, and the simplest of ideas that can be the most successful. The old adage "less is more," which was adopted by and popularized by the architect Ludwig Mies van der Rohe, is always worth bearing in mind when approaching flower design. Mies promoted clarity and simplicity to create a good architectural design. Whatever artistic medium you chose, the simplest ideas are always the best and the most enduring. Fussy or elaborate design is less visually arresting, and when it comes to working with flowers their own beauty should be the focus of any design.

When you are making a special effort for a birthday, anniversary, or wedding reception the floral decorations are just one aspect of the overall look. Ideally, I think it is best to choose the flower arrangements, then decide on the linens and the look for the table. I think it is also a good idea to decide how much you want to spend, then ask your florist or designer how best to meet the budget. It is important to decorate the tables, but often it is better to have one large arrangement than lots of little ones if funds are limited. If you are arranging the flowers yourself, then you need to be realistic about what you can achieve on your own. For events we often use whole teams of arrangers. The most important thing is that you have time to enjoy the event.

# entertaining family and friends

Producing simple flower arrangements with the minimum fuss is my aim when I am entertaining my relatives and friends. Usually I try to do my table decorations the day before, so that the flowers have time to settle and open a little for the event. Often I have two or three smaller vases down the center of a table, containing hand-tied bouquets. Daytime events and sunlight allow for lighter flower arrangements and pretty pastel colors. Artificial light and evening events demand stronger color themes.

ABOVE This low table arrangement derives its vibrant color from exotic leucospermums, viburnum berries, cotinus, celosia, gloriosa, pink germini gerberas and 'Milano', 'Orange Juice', 'Wow', and 'Supergreen' roses.

OPPOSITE Surrounding this storm lantern is a late-summer combination of *Alchemilla mollis*, *Weigela* 'Sparkling Fantasy', 'Black Baccara' and 'Mamma Mia' roses, red dahlias, 'Royal Fantasy' lilies, and *Gaillardia* 'Kobold' set in floral foam.

LEFT Pink phalaenopsis orchid heads decorate a ribbon-tied napkin, adding a jolt of deeper color in an otherwise cool scheme.

RIGHT This color-themed table includes white tulips, white phalaenopsis orchids, white ranunculus, and white lilac, used in tall and low frosted vases to create different heights. Individual places are marked with a planted snowdrop in a silver cube and a miniature succulent plant.

# dinner parties

I try to pick more dramatic color schemes or use vases that create drama, but are still intimate. If the table is long, I use a number of containers that are of differing heights but the same finish. I like clear glass because it is so versatile; colored glass also works well. Frosted glass is a current favorite, particularly when used in conjunction with white flowers.

LEFT This hand-tied posy of orange zinnias, *Achillea* 'Moonshine', 'Colandro', and 'Milano' roses, gloriosa, and celosia is arranged in a moisture-containing pink gel that is produced especially for the flower trade and looks like ice. The fluffy patches are the tops of *Cotinus*, or the smoke bush, which enhance the texture of this arrangement.

OPPOSITE Hand-tied bunches of summer flowers in peachy pink tones fill a glass trough. Pink *Astilbe* x *arendsii* 'Amerika', lime *Alchemilla mollis*, and 'Pinky Flair' hypericum contrast with the dark purple *Cotinus coggygria* 'Royal Purple'.

OPPOSITE Earthenware jars are filled with hand-tied bouquets of eryngium, marguerites, achillea, white commercially grown *Scabiosa caucasica* var. *alba*, wild *Scabiosa columbaria*, wild knapweed, and green wheat, alongside artichokes hollowed out and filled with a pillar candle.

BELOW A French white-painted wire basket is filled with *Viburnum opulus*, white lilac, white ranunculus, white bouvardia, white stocks, white 'Ice Queen' gerberas, and white tulips for a cool and smart-looking table centerpiece.

LEFT 'Princess Alexandra' garden roses are massed together in a matching rubber vase. I really enjoy mixing the old with the new by taking an old-fashioned rose and putting it into a vase made from a vibrant new material.

OPPOSITE This basket was filled with carpet moss and topped with some old garden favorites, such as *Dianthus* 'Monica Wyatt', border spray carnations, chrysanthemums, and single pink michaelmas daisies, and feverfew, *Alchemillia mollis*, and a touch of double pink eustoma.

## afternoon teas

This is a good way of having a larger, grander party on a budget, as cutting out a formal meal and alcohol helps immensely with costs. And the traditional look of chintz, pretty china, and embroidered cloths with matching slightly retro food melts the heart of the most die-hard partygoer!

LEFT This tea-table vase is filled with 'Leila' gerberas, 'Aqua!', and 'Vampire' roses, dill, peonies, *Cotinus coggygria* 'Royal Purple', celosia, red amaranthus, and sprigs of *Origanum vulgare*.

OPPOSITE A hand-tied bunch of marguerite daisies that could have come fresh from the garden are simply arranged in a terra-cotta pot that has been given an antique finish.

LEFT Pink glass flowerpots filled with hand-tied posies of sweet peas, 'Dorothy Perkins' roses, and lavender sit next to jelly jars edged with string and lined with translucent flower petals.

OPPOSITE A glass cake stand has been filled with champagne pink glass beads to hide the foam. *Viburnum opulus* 'Roseum' flower heads were laid on the napkins, and a dusting of pink rose petals were strewn across the table.

# birthdays

In each culture and country, different birthday years are considered special. In the floral business, we send flowers every day on behalf of clients commemorating birthdays who are separated by distance and cannot be together. It is usually the coming-of-age party—whether this is celebrated at sixteen, eighteen, or twenty-one—that is the first excuse for a larger family or social occasions. Table decorations vary according to the culture, location, tradition, and budget, but the one defining factor is that there are always some flowers.

An orange ceramic cube is filled with red skimmia, 'Naomi' roses, red Clooney ranunculus, and 'Palomino' roses. The flower heads are packed in tightly together to maintain a compact shape.

A stemmed glass bowl was edged with pearlized shells and filled with *Viburnum opulus*, 'Mamma Mia' and 'Contour' roses, and lilac. Pearl-headed pins are distributed throughout the arrangement for extra sparkle.

LEFT Tall pink vases with posies of three roses apiece and a collar of galax leaves decorate party tables. For significant birthdays, such as eighteenth and twenty-first, you can make a specific number of repeated arrangements like these—one for each year the host is celebrating.

OPPOSITE For an outdoor celebration, tall candelabra are filled with large-headed summer blooms, such as dahlias, hydrangeas, and *Viburnum opulus*, with long trails of amaranthus.

RIGHT Multicolored cubes stacked in different formations, like a child's wooden blocks, are decorated with roses, achillea, marguerite daisies, *Alchemilla mollis*, and sprigs of unripe blackberries.

# christenings

These are joyous celebrations and the opportunity for some fun with flowers and floral design. For the home or the party venue, we like to plan something a little whimsical and fun. Naturally, candy often plays a part, but we have used the child's building block idea several times and also made mossed ducks, teddies, and rabbits. I like to design with delicate flowers or simple shapes, either in pastel colors or primary colors. I prefer to use peach and white rather than the more stereotypical pinks and blues.

OPPOSITE The purity of white seems appropriate for christenings and is suitable for boys and girls. This all-white design of hydrangea, roses, and eustoma is set in a plain white ceramic cube.

RIGHT This orange cube, filled with *Brachyglottis* 'Sunshine', ivy berries, and 'Milva' and 'Renate' roses is equally unisex in feel.

LEFT Pale pink tulips, white sweet peas, honeysuckle, and dill in a glass vase filled with alphabet candies create a gorgeous scented spring offering. The palest pink mixes well with other pastel colors, and this is one of the rare occasions when you find me mixing pale yellow with pink.

OPPOSITE A gingham-covered basket is filled with cream 'Gracia' and pink 'Mimi Eden' spray roses, feverfew, *Brachyglottis* 'Sunshine', and *Alchemilla mollis*—the perfect theme to welcome a baby girl.

LEFT This square wreath is very easy to make but can be time consuming. Ribbon is wound round a mossed wire frame, then cranberries are fixed in place individually with pearl-headed pins.

OPPOSITE It is amazing how long a simple foliage arrangement lasts. Ivy, holly, photinia, and *Brachyglottis* 'Sunshine' look festive with just a few ribbon bows. The suspended wreath is made from dried pomegranates glued onto a straw frame.

# christmas

Although I am always at my busiest at Christmastime, I adore the tradition of decorating my home. I love the pagan idea of filling the house with greenery and dragging in a huge tree. Having decorated many spaces for Christmas, I can say that this is a time when excess is the only word. The great thing is that it need not be expensive if you have access to some foliage—plenty of greenery is key to making a good show. A little bit of spray paint helps, a roll or two of ribbon, a handful of cones, some fruits, maybe some spices, and off you go!

LEFT Low trays were filled with foam and covered with pine, orange cotoneaster berries, brown-berried hypericum, and *Brachyglottis*. Cones and cinnamon give texture and scent, and bright green hellebores and 'Black Baccara' and 'Léonidas' roses add color. Piles of fruit, cones, and cinnamon decorate the surrounding table.

OPPOSITE A plastic bowl was surrounded with stems of *Ilex* x *meserveae* 'Blue Prince', secured on with double-sided tape and tied with cord. A foam block holds waxed and glittered apples, gold taper candles, and 'Black Baccara', 'Naomi', and 'Cherry Brandy' roses.

**OPPOSITE** Winter whites set the tone for a sparkling Christmas. One tall silver vase is topped with a floral-foam ball covered with ivy berries, ranunculus, silver-sprayed eryngium, lilac, 'Avalanche+' roses, and astilbe, with jasmine trails. Silver beakers are filled with astilbe, ranunculus, and hellebores.

**THIS PAGE** The napkin decoration is a silver-sprayed pinecone nestled in a delicate jasmine sprig.

Topiary lavender trees in gray ceramic cubes have been sprayed with glitter. Garlands of silvered ivy trails are pinned to the tablecloth, with pink organza bows with added crystals for a sparkly effect. Mirrored votives fill the table—some hold posies of 'Sweet Avalanche+' roses and *Acacia baileyana* 'Purpurea' while others contain silver-sprayed crab apples.

OPPOSITE Three hand-tied bouquets of 'Aqua!', 'Black Baccara', and 'Colandro' roses mixed with bunches of red skimmia are set in pink cubes repeated to form a centerpiece down the length of the table.

RIGHT Delicate Moroccan tea glasses are filled with small posies of the same flowers to mark individual place settings.

LEFT A natural-feeling and loose-hanging wreath uses a range of seasonal greenery, including *Garrya elliptica*, cotoneaster, ivy berries, larch, and lichen, along with red berries and red skimmia for holiday glory.

OPPOSITE Wreaths are very versatile and make pretty decorations suspended on chains or ribbons. Trailing ivy and larch stems are interspersed with hypericum berries, burgundy carnations, and hanging green amaranthus.

LEFT Moss topiaries are more time consuming than foam ones to make, but the reward is in the longevity of the design. Blue spruce, variegated holly, *Viburnum tinus* berries, and ivy berries are studded with limes and a selection of dried seed heads, cones, and starfish sprayed silver.

OPPOSITE Using different textures, some artificial and some natural, on a base of blue spruce has created a monochromatic wreath. The circular movement of the ribbon helps to make it look more harmonious.

RIGHT Frosted vases of different heights have been used to decorate an ivory and gold wedding table. The simple use of different vases of all one type of flower gives a sumptuous look. The peony chair backs are tied with organza ribbon. On the side table are vases of flocked Sumatra twigs, massed hydrangea, and white everlasting sweet pea.

# weddings

Flowers are central to weddings and are often one of the things we remember long after other components have been forgotten. Brides tell me it was the best day of their lives, and I can bump into ex-clients decades after their big day and we can spend hours reliving it! When it comes to floral decorations, the possibilities are endless and limited only by budget. Expense, though, is not always key; I have been involved in sumptuous weddings that have lacked the intimacy, flair, and generosity to be found in more modest affairs.

LEFT A dome of white 'Avalanche+' roses has been arranged in a glass cylinder lined with slices of kiwi fruit for a summer centerpiece.

OPPOSITE Massed balls of *Chrysanthemum* 'White Reagan' are interspersed with silver candelabras adorned with daisy garlands, which also snake along the table. A single stemmed flower sits on each napkin.

# wedding tables

The main determination for your table decoration will be the budget and timing of the celebration. Outdoor weddings and garden parties will suggest very different table decorations from ballrooms and internal venues. Daylight allows for much softer flowers and designs than evening events. Candlelight always seems to play some essential part, either at the ceremony or on the tables.

These low wedding table arrangements were made out of baskets covered in lichen twigs and moss and filled with hydrangea, ivy berries, *Brachyglottis* 'Sunshine', and 'Metallina', 'Vendella', 'Talea+', and 'Old Dutch' roses. Woven throughout the design are trails of scented stephanotis.

A metal frame holds five night-lights, with a leaf-covered bowl placed in the middle. This summer arrangement uses white peonies, with 'Margaret Merril', 'Julia's Baby', and 'Vendella' roses, cream double eustoma, white sweet pea, *Alchemilla mollis*, variegated weigela, and *Eucalyptus parvifolia*.

Marla

OPPOSITE A floral-foam ring around a pink glass candelabra is edged with *Alchemilla mollis* and ivy berries topped with pink and burgundy dahlias, with bright pink 'Karl Rosenfield' peonies, 'Milano' roses, and gloriosa lilies.

RIGHT A three-tier hexagonal pink wedding cake has been interspersed with two blocks of floral foam, separated from the icing on the cake by clear cellophane to avoid any contamination of the food. The foam holds 'Blushing Akito', 'Belle Rose', 'Heaven!', 'Aqua!', and 'Lyveria!' standard roses and the deep pink spray rose 'Magic Pepita'.

## chair backs

These are little bouquets that can be added to the back or side of a chair, or can be hung on the pews at a church or religious venue. Their increased popularity is due to the fact that they look casual, are relatively inexpensive, and are very useful for marking an aisle at any civil ceremony venue.

OPPOSITE Garden roses, hydrangea, and *Brachyglottis* 'Sunshine' have been tied together and attached to chair backs to decorate the seating at the head table for this reception.

LEFT A hand-tied bunch of white marguerite daisies (*Argyranthemum frutescens*) secured with a natural raffia bow makes a charming decoration with a country feel for a summer wedding.

BELOW LEFT One perfect flower head of white *Hydrangea macrophylla* 'Schneeball' ia a suitably minimalistic adornment for this classic designer chair.

LEFT White is the classic color choice in this bridal bouquet of pure white 'Akito' roses hand-tied with *Bouvardia* 'Diamond White'.

OPPOSITE The muted dusty rose–pink shades of *Zantedeschia* 'Aurora', cream 'Talea+' roses, and pink *Astilbe* 'Erica' are perfect for lifting the bouquet from the wedding gown and creating a subtle yet warm, rosy glow.

# bridal bouquets

These are the stars of the wedding flowers and should reflect the personality of the bride and complement her dress. The best way to ensure a good match is for the bride to take a few flowers when she is having a dress fitting and view herself in a mirror. Florists are often happy to make up a miniature bouquet to take along.

This rich bouquet was created for a bride who chose deep purple for her wedding gown. The design includes 'Black Baccara' and 'Milano' roses, *Viburnum opulus*, and purple eustoma.

A summer wedding allows the greatest choice of flowers for the bridal bouquet, including lilac, sweet peas, and garden roses, which are at their best and most plentiful between June and September.

I love to do two- or three-color bouquets for spring and summer weddings. *Muscari* is a beautiful wedding flower as its shape is so delicate. Here it is combined with 'Blushing Akito' roses and blue nigella.

This generous hand-tied bridal bouquet is composed of pink veronica, *Alchemilla mollis*, echinops, 'Sarah Bernhardt' peonies, white scabious, 'Cool Water!' roses, and gray amaranthus.

LEFT Generally speaking a boutonniere can be made from any type of flower, but there are some that are far more popular because they are inexpensive and wire well. Carnations are popular as they last well; this red carnation is edged with lime hypericum berries and foliage.

OPPOSITE, FROM TOP LEFT Orchids are very successful but tend to be more expensive to purchase; this green cymbidium orchid is edged with camellia leaves. A speckled phalaenopsis orchid has lily grass loops and camellia leaves. Hebe and gloriosa with grass loops have a binding of decorative pink floral wire rather than the usual green ribbon.

## boutonnieres

There is something gallant about men wearing boutonnieres, and women can wear them attached to hats, handbags, or pinned to their hair if dresses are too delicate to support a wired flower. Any flower can, in theory, be wired, but something robust is less likely to end up as a pressed flower!

# techniques

OPPOSITE For larger vases, baskets, and also large pedestals, I use 2-inch chicken wire to arrange flowers. I scrunch the wire up so that it fits the container so tightly you can pick up the vase by the wire, then I push the flower stems through the wire.

**the essential techniques** of designing with flowers fall into two distinct categories: floristry and flower arranging. Traditionally amateur flower arranging, pursued either for the enjoyment of a hobby or for social or charity pursuits, involved arranging flowers originally in chicken wire and later in floral foam and rarely involved wiring, which was seen as a floristry technique.

Floristry was seen more as the domain of the professionals, the commercial flower shops. Here you would find skilled florists who could make a wired shower bouquet or a three-dimensional sympathy tribute from flower heads. Now these two areas have become more blurred and fall under the general category of floral design. Many florists are working without an outlet or a shop, and many flower arrangers offer a wider range of skills. Recently, cut flowers have also been given a wider commercial arena, with a much greater variety being offered in supermarkets and even gas stations, and also for sale on the Internet at very competitive prices, making the industry even more fragmented. The original floristry techniques for producing formal displays have decreased in demand as tastes have changed, and it is now much harder to learn these skills as an apprentice, which had formally been the most common way of honing your art or trade.

All of the essential techniques required for arranging flowers well are laid out in the following pages in a series of easy-to-follow step-by-step projects. The core of any flower design is, of course, the flowers themselves, so it is essential to make sure the flowers are well looked after, conditioned, and the best quality.

1

2

3

# hand-tied bouquets

These take some time to perfect, but will hugely widen your versatility as a flower arranger. It is best to start with some straight, reasonably robust flowers. Smaller posies are easier than long-stemmed flowers so try to build confidence with this simple but effective design.

## you will need

- 15 'Versilla' roses
- 10 dark red 'Viking' dahlias
- 10 calla lilies (*Zantedeschia* 'Chopin')
- 10 *Asclepias* 'Alessa'
- 10 stems of *Ajania pacifica* 'Silver and Gold'
- 3 bunches of *Panicum virgatum* 'Squaw'
- 10 stems of *Achillea* 'Moonshine'
- 10 stems of *Astrantia major* 'Claret'
- 5 stems of *Eryngium* 'Orion Questar'
- 10 stems of *Nectaroscordum siculum*
- 5 bunches of *Galax urceolata* leaves
- a sharp knife
- a roll of florists' bind wire
- a long glass trough

**1** To make hand-tied posies, it is very important to cut down the flowers and foliage and clean any foliage from below the head of the stem. When all the plant material has been stripped, lay out the flowers in neat piles of the same variety. As this is going to be a very small posy, you will need to hold the plant material at the top of the stem near the head. Take a strong central flower, such as a rose, then place further plant material to the left of the first flower until you have created a small fan of plant material. At this stage, you need to twist the flowers, taking them into your other hand, then add five more stems. Keep spiraling and twisting until you have fifteen stems in each bunch, including three roses.

**2** Add the galax leaves to the edge to create a collar. It is essential the stems are clean so that when you tie them at the binding point, the lower area is free from debris and the water will not get contaminated. Tie firmly with florists' bind wire. Continue making four more bunches in the same way.

**3** Re-cut the stems and place the posies into the trough using the galax collar to keep them in place. Fill the trough with water and flower food.

1

2

3

4

# victorian posy

The key here is to use the right plant material, and I think spring flowers are ideal. The stems are thinner, so you will need to perfect the art of the light touch or you will find they break. Turn the posy with the addition of every flower so that you work evenly all around.

### you will need

- a central rose
- 2 bunches of forget-me-nots
- 12 'Vendella' roses
- 3 bunches of sweet peas
- 10 bunches of *Muscari*
- strong twine
- ribbon

**1** First clean all the foliage and thorns from the roses, and clean the forget-me-nots. Carefully arrange the forget-me-nots around the central rose in your left hand. Keep turning the bunch with your right hand as you are doing this so you can make a neat circle of blue flowers around the central single rose.

**2** Next add the 'Vendella' roses just a little lower than the height of the forget-me-nots—creating the domed shape. Make sure that you place the roses at exactly the same height all around to create a defined circular shape.

**3** Next, you are ready to add the delicate sweet peas. Keep your left hand very relaxed as you add them, then use your right hand to move the bunch so that you are working on all sides.

**4** Finally, add bunches of five muscari at a time, placing them lower than the sweet peas. Work around three times in all (adding three layers of the grape hyacinths) so that you have a sumptuously bunched finished effect. Tie tightly with twine, then finish with decorative ribbon.

1

2

3

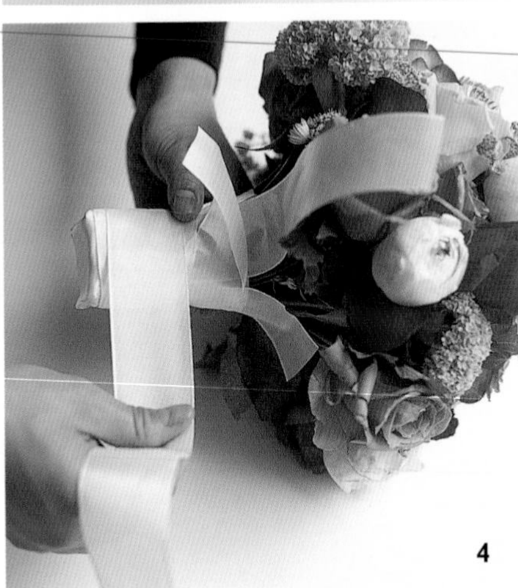
4

# rose dome bouquet

It is imperative that all the stems go in the same direction in this posy, and no stem should ever cross another. Make sure you hold the bunch loosely, and remember to keep turning it as you work, always placing the flowers in at the same side and same angle.

## you will need

- 40 garden roses in mixed colors
- a sharp knife
- 5 stems of *Viburnum opulus*
- string
- a pair of scissors
- green gutta-percha tape
- a roll of double-sided tape
- ribbon

**1** First clean your roses and remove all the lower foliage. Strip the rose stems of thorns. Take a sharp knife and gently pry them off by moving the blade down the length of the stem.

**2** Take a central rose and, holding it between your thumb and first finger, add flowers at an angle to the left-hand side. Add about five flowers, then twist the bunch, using your right hand to move it but keeping it in your left hand. Add five more flowers and twist again.

**3** Tie your posy tightly underneath the flower heads with string so that it is firmly held together, then trim all the stems to the width of your hand. Tie again at the bottom of the stems to form the handle, then, starting from the base of the heads, bind to the tip with the green gutta-percha tape.

**4** To hide the stems, run double-sided tape down either side and cover lengthwise with two to four strips of ribbon. Add another strip around the handle, working from the top to the bottom and then back to the top. Secure with a bow made from three loops and one central ribbon.

1

## you will need

- 10 stems of Clooney ranunculus
- a bunch of pink jasmine
- 2 bunches of pink sweet peas
- 2 bunches of purple sweet peas
- 5 'Sarah Bernhardt' peonies
- 8 stems of astrantia
- a selection of different-size florists' wires
- a roll of silver wire
- a roll of green stem tape
- a pack of lilac skeletonized leaves
- pink ribbon
- a pearl-headed pin

2 3

# wired bouquet

This is the hardest bouquet to make. You will need to be proficient in wiring to begin, so it is best to practice the technique first. This bouquet would take at least an hour to make if you are competent and fast, and may take half a day or more if you are still gaining experience.

**1** Remove all the flower heads from their stems, and wire them using the appropriate size florists' wire. The larger heads should be wired internally by placing the wire into the stem and up into the flower head. With the delicate stems of jasmine, sweet pea, and astrantia, place a thin silver wire through a stem and loop one length of the wire over the other and the stem three times to form a double-leg mount. Cover the wire with stem tape.

**2** Place all the flowers into a round posy shape. Take care not to cross your wires and use a mirror to check the shape. Wire the skeletonized leaves with a double-leg mount and place them around the bouquet; bind with silver wire.

**3** Bind down the stem with a ribbon held at a slight diagonal, then continue back up the other side and secure with a pearl-headed pin pushed into the center of the bouquet and/or by tying on a bow.

## you will need

- a stand and amphora
- a plastic bucket
- a length of chicken wire
- 10 stems of flowering *Photinia fraseri* 'Red Robin'
- 10 tall branches of *Sorbus aria* 'Majestica'
- 5 long branches of rhododendron
- 10 tall branches of *Prunus* 'Sato-zakura'
- 10 stems of long *Ruscus hypophyllum*
- 10 stems of Solomon's seal (*Polygonatum*)
- 10 stems of weeping willow
- 10 stems of lilac (*Syringa vulgaris* 'Dark Koster')
- 10 stems of *Viburnum opulus* 'Roseum'
- 10 stems of *Moluccella laevis*
- 10 stems of *Antirrhinum majus* 'Potomac Rose'
- 15 stems of larkspur (*Delphinium consolida* 'Pink Perfection')
- 5 white *Delphinium elatum* 'Snow Queen Arrow'
- 10 *Lilium* 'Sorbonne'
- 15 stems of *Paeonia* 'Red Charm'

# freestanding pot

If you want to make larger arrangements, then it is easier to create it in a round, freestanding container like this than to make a traditional front-facing arrangement. It might take slightly more flowers and foliage, but the result is more natural and it is a lot easier to achieve.

**1** Line the pot with a plastic bucket. Use some scrunched-up chicken wire to enable the pot to sit flush within the container. Fill with water, mixed with flower food.

**2** Using a mixture of the different foliage, create the outline of the arrangement you wish to make. For a large freestanding arrangement, the flowers should be one and a half times the height of the container.

**3** For a round arrangement, all the stems should radiate from a central point. Once you have a good base and structure with the foliage, you can start to add the flowers, beginning with the *Prunus*.

**4** Use trailing foliage, such as the ruscus, Solomon's seal, and willow, to trail down over the front of the pot.

**5** Next add all the woody stems, such as the lilac and the viburnum, and all the tall spires, such as *Moluccella*, antirrhinum, larkspur, and delphinium. Finally, add the star-shaped lilies throughout the arrangement at different heights and depths, then place the peonies to fill in any gaps.

1

2

## you will need

- a conical topiary frame
- a bale of sphagnum moss
- a length of chicken wire
- a roll of heavy florists' wire
- a metal urn
- 2 bunches of *Camellia japonica*
- 10 stems of *Forsythia intermedia* 'Spectabilis'
- a selection of wires
- 5 bunches of *Narcissus tazetta* 'Laurens Koster'
- 5 bunches of orange *Ranunculus* 'Ranobelle Inra Zalm'
- 50 stems of yellow *Calendula officianalis* 'Greenheart Orange'
- 50 stems of *Rosa* 'Lemonade'
- 50 stems of *Rosa* 'Milva'
- 30 stems of *Leucospermum cordifolium* 'Fireball'
- 30 sharon fruit

3

4

5

# conical topiary

This sumptuous-looking topiary is a detailed, extravagant design created for special occasions. We use this kind of design when we want to create giant arrangements, or when we want to use a mixture of fruit and flowers and need a firm base on which to fix the plant material.

**1** Stuff the topiary frame with the sphagnum moss so that it forms a very firm base.

**2** Line the mossed cone with chicken wire, using the florists' wire to bind it onto the frame.Then wire it into the metal urn so that it is very stable.

**3** Cover the frame with small sprigs of camellia foliage inserted into the moss. Then arrange the ten stems of forsythia into the bottom of the urn and place them vertically around the frame so that they all meet at the top. Secure them with hairpin bends of heavy stub wire.

**4** Next prepare all your flowers. Wire them by placing a heavy stub wire up the stem and into the flower head. Take one wire and pass it through the bottom of a sharon fruit, then pass another wire through at right angles to the first. At this stage, the wires resemble a cross. Bend them all down together at the bottom of the sharon fruit and twist so that the four wire legs become one. Trim the wires to 2 inches.

**5** Push the wired sharon fruit into the moss, evenly spaced. Add all the wired flowers, placing the narcissi last as they are the most delicate.

# trailing arrangement

This style of arrangement is useful for front-facing tables at weddings, or for window ledges and mantelpieces. If you are using a light plastic spray tray, as shown here, do make sure that your flowers and foliage are well balanced, both physically and aesthetically.

## you will need

- 2 blocks of floral foam
- a long spray tray
- a roll of floral-foam tape
- 20 stems of Solomon's seal (*Polygonatum multiflorum*)
- 10 stems of fountain grass (*Panicum* 'Fountain')
- 10 stems of *Alchemilla mollis*
- 10 stems of *Viburnum opulus*
- 10 stems of *Lupinus* 'Little Eugenie'
- 10 stems of peach spray roses
- 10 stems of *Rosa* 'Vendella'
- 10 stems of *Rosa* 'Peach'
- 7 stems of *Paeonia lactiflora* 'Sorbet'
- 10 stems of astilbe

**1** Soak the floral foam in water until the bubbles cease rising, then place the foam blocks on a flat white spray tray and tape them down. Trim the corner of the foam to help with placing the material. It is always best to make this kind of arrangement in situ. Place the tray at the front of the table and start to create the outline by using the trailing stems of Solomon's seal.

**2** Next add the fountain grass evenly throughout the design.

**3** Fill out the design by using the *Alchemilla mollis* and *Viburnum opulus*, then place seven of the lupins through the design as your longest flowers.

**4** Using the spray roses and the standard roses, fill out the design, then place the open peonies in the most prominent positions. These central flowers will be the area that the eye is drawn to, which is known as the focal point.

**5** Fill any gaps with the astilbe, working from the trailing edge through to the edge of the foam on the other side. Although these arrangements are often viewed from the front, make sure they also look good from the back if they will be viewed from there, for instance, on a wedding head table.

1

2

3

4

# oval table center

This traditional centerpiece is often described as a long and low arrangement. Its raised profile and diamond footprint is the basic form used for sympathy sprays. The outline is established with foliage, and it is better to use lots of different types to get a soft and interesting look.

## you will need

- 2 blocks of floral foam
- a 12-inch-long rectangular container
- 2 green bamboo skewers
- a roll of floral tape
- a tall pillar candle
- a bunch of ivy trails
- a bunch of fruiting ivy
- a bunch of witch hazel (*Hamamelis virginiana*)
- 5 stems of *Viburnum opulus*
- a bunch of white *Ranunculus* 'Ranobelle Inra Wit'
- a bunch of *Tulipa* 'Winterberg'
- 7 *Rosa* 'Alexis'
- 7 *Rosa* 'Avalanche+'
- 5 stems of lilac (*Syringa vulgaris* 'Madame Florent Stepman')

**1** Soak the floral foam blocks in water and arrange them in the rectangular container so that the foam is at least an inch above the edge of the container. Cut the green bamboo skewers to create four legs and tape these onto the bottom of the candle. Press the candle down in the center of the arrangement so that it is firmly anchored.

**2** Next take the ivy trails and help establish the flowing outline of the arrangement, using the longer pieces at either end of the arrangement. Use ivy berries to create a diamond-shaped base for your flowers.

**3** Add branches of the witch hazel and the *Viburnum opulus* through the arrangement to create movement and to add interest.

**4** Taking each individual flower, place it through the center of the arrangement at different heights and depths, using a zigzag motion from left to right. Fill in any gaps with sprigs of white lilac.

1

2 3

# topiary candelabra

Covering a basic candelabra with plant material can give it a completely new and sculptural look. Sometimes we use foliage material, such as hebe, rosemary, box, or pussy willow. Cut twigs, such as flowering blossom, also work well, or dried, painted, or dyed material.

1

## you will need

- a metal 5-prong candelabra
- 2 bunches of painted birch twigs
- a roll of heavy blue wire
- a block of floral foam
- a roll of florists' pot tape
- a 20-inch floral-foam ring
- a bunch of berried ivy
- a bunch of *Brachyglottis* 'Sunshine'
- a bunch of *Hebe albicans* 'Red Edge'
- 5 stems of hydrangea
- 7 stems of *Agapanthus* 'Atlantic Ocean'
- 10 stems of stocks (*Matthiola incana* 'Centum Lavender')
- 15 stems of *Eustoma russellium* 'Fuji Silver Blue'
- 32 stems of *Rosa* 'Sterling Silver'
- 5 taper candles

2

3

**1** Bind the stem of the candelabra with the birch twigs using wire. Soak the floral foam blocks in water, then place it into the center of the candelabra, and tape it into place with pot tape. Soak the floral ring and stand it around the base of the candelabra. Trim off the edge of the foam to make it easier to add the plant material. Paring a little off the edge and smoothing the shape is sometimes referred to as "chamfering."

**2** Place the ivy in the floral foam, working from all angles to create a loose shape, including some trails down the candelabra. Fill in with *Brachyglottis* and hebe to give a good outline and shape. Fill the ring with foliage so you cover the floral foam.

**3** Starting with the largest flowers position the hydrangea flower heads around the candelabra. For the top arrangement, you should be aiming for a ball shape. Continue to build the shape with the agapanthus, stock, and eustoma. Repeat the process with the remaining flowers to fill the floral foam ring at the base. Finally, place your roses in pairs throughout the arrangement and complete by adding in your candles.

## you will need

- a round basket
- a round plastic pot
- a length of chicken wire
- a roll of florists' wire
- a bunch of berried ivy
- a bunch of *Brachyglottis* 'Sunshine'
- 5 stems of *Viburnum opulus* 'Roseum'
- 5 stems of lilac (*Syringa vulgaris* 'Dark Koster')
- 10 stems of *Scilla sibirica*
- 10 stems of *Tulipa* 'Blue Diamond'
- 10 stems of *Argyranthemum frutescens*
- 20 stems of forget-me-nots

# wire-filled basket

Baskets are a staple of the floral industry. You can fill them with floral foam or use chicken wire, as here. All flowers last longer in water rather than floral foam, so I use this method when the flowers are delicate, the weather is hot, or the arrangement needs longevity.

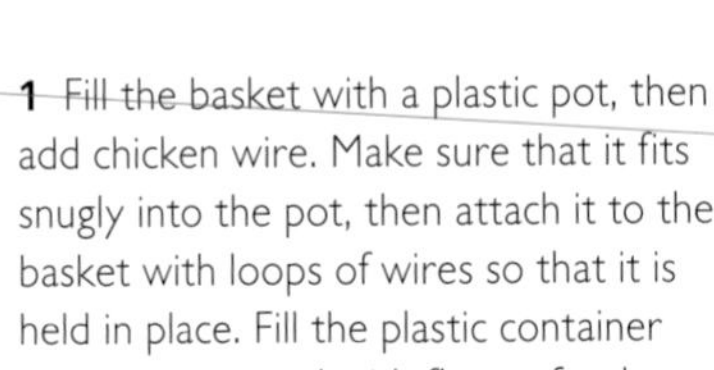

**1** Fill the basket with a plastic pot, then add chicken wire. Make sure that it fits snugly into the pot, then attach it to the basket with loops of wires so that it is held in place. Fill the plastic container with water mixed with flower food.

**2** For most of my designs, a third of the plant material will be foliage, and I usually like to select at least three different varieties to create a good base for the flowers. Start by adding the ivy, then the *Brachyglottis*, then the lime green balls of the *Viburnum opulus*.

**3** When the chicken wire is covered, you can begin to add the flowers. It is best to start with the woody stemmed flowers, such as the flowering lilac, and the heavy bulb stems, such as the scillas.

**4** Then add the tulips, taking care to make sure that all the stems radiate from the central point and that each flower is represented throughout the arrangement at different heights and depths to create a natural effect. Finally, add the delicate flowers, such as the daisies and the forget-me-nots.

1

2

3

## you will need

- 2 blocks of floral foam
- a glass vase
- a roll of pot tape
- a bamboo cane
- a selection of heavy stub wires
- a burgundy pillar candle
- a bunch of berried ivy
- a bunch of *Skimmia japonica* 'Rubella'
- 5 stems of hypericum
- 8 small waxed pears
- a stem of cymbidium orchid
- 7 *Rosa* 'Grand Prix'

4

# candle centerpiece

This simple design is an easy gift or table center for any season. Make sure you use as much foam as you can in the container and that it is at least 2 inches above the edge. This supports the heavy candle and gives more surface area in which to display greenery and flowers.

**1** After soaking the floral foam, place one and a half blocks vertically in the container. It is important that the foam is above the edge of the container so that you can create a rounded shape. Secure it with pot tape. Cut a bamboo cane into four or make hairpins with the heavy wire. Tape the canes or wires to the bottom of your candle so that you can anchor it into the foam.

**2** Starting with the ivy berries, place small sprigs around the foam at different heights and depths. Next add the skimmia and the hypericum berries, spreading them evenly.

**3** Take one wire and pass it through the bottom of a waxed pear, then pass another wire through at right angles to the first. At this stage, the wires resemble a cross. Bend them all down together at the bottom of the pear and twist so that the four wire legs become one. Trim the wires to 1½ inches. If you cannot get waxed pears use natural ones or spray paint them for more color.

**4** Take the orchid and cut it into three pieces. Place it into the foam, then add the roses at different heights and depths around the vase. Finally anchor the wires of the pears firmly into the foam.

# lined glass cubes

The 6-inch glass vase is my all-time favorite vase for creating a variety of modest and accessible arrangements. The use of an inner liner allows you to use either foam or water and prevents the flowers from being contaminated by your choice of decoration for the outer chamber.

### you will need

- 4 4½-inch glass cubes
- 4 6-inch glass cubes
- 50 stems of pussy willow
- scissors
- 30 stems of white 'Carnegie' hyacinths
- 50 stems of ranunculus
- 50 stems of 'Weber's Parrot' tulips
- 30 stems of white lilac
- string

**1** Place one of the smaller vases inside one of the larger vases and fill the gap with 5½-inch lengths of pussy willow.

**2** Complete each set of four vases in the same way, and trim the willow so that it is flush with the top of the vases. Strip all the lower foliage from the stems of the flowers, then spiral them into hand-tied bouquets. Tie with string. Fill the center of the vase with water and trim the bouquet to fit. Repeat with the three other flowers, using a single type of flower for each bouquet.

**3** When the flowers are fitting snugly in the container, cut the string to loosen up the flower heads so that they cover the tops of the two vases.

1

2

3

### you will need

- a roll of double-sided tape
- 3 glass votives
- 2 branches of laurel
- 6 stems of variegated pittosporum
- a bunch of snowdrops
- a bunch of hellebores
- 3 stems of catkins
- a bunch of aconites
- 6 stems of *Viburnum* x *bodnantense*
- string

**1** First place some double-sided tape all around the votives. Stick some laurel leaves all around the edge of the glass votives in an upright fashion, overlapping them slightly.

**2** Trim the bottom off the leaves so they are flush with the votive, then fill the glass with water. It is always a good idea to add some flower food, particularly for fragile cut garden flowers such as the ones used here.

**3** Trim the lower foliage from the stems of the flowers and foliages, cut them to the same length, and then hand tie into small posies. Secure them with string. Once tied, cut the stems again to fit snugly into the leaved votives.

# wrapped vases

Adapting containers with plant material, such as glossy leaves, is easy, and creates a sculptural and effective result. It is also economical, making the most of recycled glass pots or jars or inexpensive but unattractive plastic pots.

1
2
3

# suspended orchids

There is an increasing trend for deconstructed arrangements where the hardware is more dominant than the flowers. These more urban-feeling designs make clever use of just a few flower heads and colored aluminum wire.

### you will need

- 2 or 3 stems of matching cymbidium orchids
- a length of colored aluminum florists' wire
- a glass vase, 3 feet tall and around 8–10 inches wide

**1** Usually there are about seven heads on each stem of a cymbidium orchid, so you will need at least two stems for this design. Remove the flower heads from the main stem, leaving a very short stalk. Next cut some lengths of the aluminum wire and twist it into curls to place inside the vase.

**2** To fill the vase, start with a coil of aluminum wire, placing it at the base of the vase. Next add some cymbidium heads, followed by further coils of aluminum wire, then continue alternating flowers and wire until you have filled the entire vase. Fill the vase to the top with water mixed with flower food so all the flower heads can absorb the water.

1

2

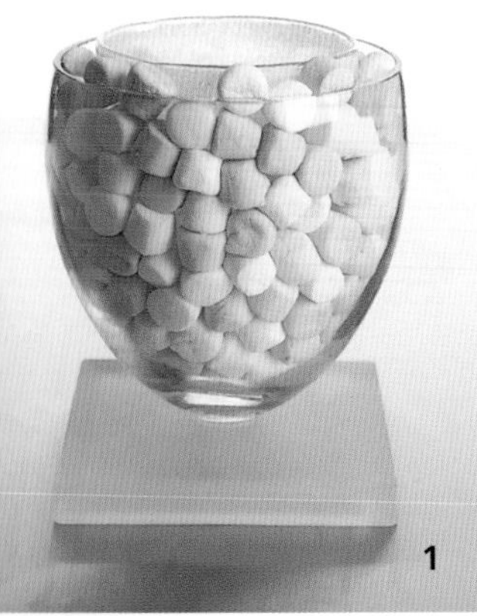

1

# lined glass urn

This classic urn is an excellent shape and is given a more contemporary look by using one smaller inner column vase to hold the bouquet of flowers. Between the vase and the outer container you can add accessories to create a sculptural feel.

2

3

4

5

## you will need

- a large, clear glass urn with a frosted plinth
- a bag of marshmallows
- a frosted glass vase
- 10 stems of *Rosa* 'Marshmallow'
- a bunch of *Camellia japonica*
- a bunch of *Viburnum tinus*
- a bunch of *Ranunculus* 'Cappuccino Pink'
- 12 stems of *Rosa* 'Barbie'
- 10 stems of *Tulipa* 'First Class'
- a length of florists' bind wire
- a pair of scissors

**1** Fill the bottom of the urn with marshmallows. Place the frosted glass vase into the center of it, then stuff the sides with more marshmallows.

**2** Taking a central 'Marshmallow' rose and a piece of foliage, start placing plant material to the left of the central rose at an angle of about 25 degrees.

**3** Add a sprig of *Viburnum tinus*, a ranunculus, a 'Barbie' rose, and a tulip, all slightly to the left of the piece before. At this point, you need to turn it in your hand, so take your right hand and twist it.

**4** Place the flowers and foliage at the same angle. Continue adding and twisting every five or six pieces of plant material. The stems should start to fan out and you will see the spiraled stem of the posy.

**5** Continue until you have used all the plant material. As the bunch starts to grow, the flowers and foliage will be placed at more of a 45-degree angle. Using the florists' bind wire, bind and tie tightly where you have been holding the bunch. Trim all the stems with a diagonal cut; if the bouquet is well balanced, it will stand on its own stems.

**6** Fill the central vase with water, and place the bouquet in the center of the vase. Gently cut the binding point so that the flowers loosen up a little bit and just fall over the edge of the vase.

### you will need

- a stemmed glass bowl
- 175 bunches of flexigrass (*Xanthorrhoea australis*)
- a roll of tape
- 16–20 bunches of *Muscari*

**1** Line the glass bowl with vertical swirls of flexigrass so that it fits snugly all around the edge. Using single lengths of floral foam or clear tape, make lines in one direction first, then across in the other direction to create a grid of tape with holes around ¾ inch square.

**2** Fill with water mixed with flower food, which will keep the water clean and free from bacteria. This is very important when you are using plant material such as the flexigrass below the water line. Working from one side of the bowl, place small bunches of *Muscari* into each square until you cover the whole grid.

# fixing with tape

When you have a small or shallow vase or something precious, such as an antique cut-glass bowl, a grid of tape is great device for arranging flowers without damaging the vase. Clear sticky tape works well, but you can also use floral-foam tape, which is more robust when in contact with moisture than ordinary tape.

# horizontal lining

For long or round arrangements, it is often best to use a horizontal lining to give the arrangement movement or to move the eye visually across the table. Spring and fall are the best times to use twigs in this way, as this is the time when the branches are most pliable.

## you will need

- 20 stems of pussy willow (*Salix caprea*)
- a 12-inch straight-sided glass bowl
- 2 blocks of floral foam
- a bunch of *Brachyglottis* 'Sunshine'
- a bunch of ivy
- a bunch of *Camellia japonica*
- 5 stems of *Viburnum opulus* 'Roseum'
- 5 stems of lilac (*Syringa vulgaris* 'Dark Koster')
- 5 stems of *Hyacinthus orientalis* 'Annalisa'
- 10 stems of *Tulipa* 'Negrita'
- 10 stems of *Ranunculus* 'Ranobelle Inra Wit'
- 10 stems of *Veronica* 'Dark Martje'
- 10 stems of *Anemone coronaria* 'Mona Lisa Blue'

1

2

3

**1** Wind the pussy willow around the inside edge of the glass bowl. Place one block of soaked foam into the center of the bowl, then cut the other block into two halves and place around the side so that it fits snugly and the foam is an inch or so above the edge of the glass container.

**2** Add foliage to the floral foam by using the small sprigs of the three varieties of the foliage, making sure they all radiate from the central point.

**3** Next add the five stems of *Viburnum opulus* and lilac, then the more delicate flowers, such as the hyacinths, tulips, ranunculus, and veronica.

**4** Finally add the anemones, placing them at different heights and depths evenly throughout the arrangement.

# basket-weave lining

The inspiration for this weave came from a trip to Thailand where you see the Thai people casually weaving leaves into a variety of shapes and designs. It takes a little patience, and often a little help from a staple gun to help you get going, but once you start, it is like knitting—quite addictive!

### you will need

- 50 stems of *Phormium tenax* 'Variegatum'
- an 8-inch glass cube
- 2 blocks of floral foam
- 20 stems of contorted willow
- 15 stems of camellia
- 15 stems of *Leucospermum cordifolium* 'Coral'
- 10 stems of *Rosa* 'Macarena'
- 10 stems of *Eustoma russellianum* 'King Violet'
- 10 stems of *Hypericum* 'Dolly Parton'
- 10 *Strelitzia reginae*

**1** Lay out six stems of *Phormium tenax* horizontally, then weave another six stems vertically through, to create a basket-weave effect. If you find it difficult to keep the leaves in place, you can use a staple gun to hold the bottom and top leaves in position.

**2** Trim to fit neatly into the glass cube. Completely fill the container with floral foam, and make sure that the foam is at least 2 inches above the edge of the container.

**3** Add the willow throughout the arrangement, then green up the base with camellia followed by groups of leucospermums, roses, eustoma, and hypericum. Finally, add the strelitzia so that they are all pointing outward from the center of the arrangement.

# wired fruit basket

The technique is very simple but the preparation does take a little time. Fruit wired like this will last up to a week in the summer if you do not bruise it too much and far longer in winter—though in the summer and fall fruits are more plentiful and inexpensive.

## you will need

- 30 Washington red apples
- a roll of florists' wire
- a sturdy basket and plastic bowl
- 4 blocks of green floral foam
- a roll of florists' pot tape
- sphagnum moss
- a bunch of ivy berries
- 10 stems of *Skimmia japonica* 'Rubella'
- 5 stems of American oak (*Quercus palustris*)
- 5 stems of golden holly berries
- 7 stems of *Leucospermum cordifolium* 'Succession'
- 10 stems of *Rudbeckia hirta*
- 15 *Rosa* 'Ruby Red'
- 15 *Rosa* 'Aqua'

**1** Wire up the apples by pushing a length of florists' wire through the lower half of the fruit so that an equal amount protrudes from each side. Next push a second wire in the other direction through the lower part of the fruit, then twist all four wires together, leaving two wire stems which can be used to attach the apple to the basket frame.

**2** Starting with the bottom layer, attach fifteen apples around the edge of the basket. When you have completed the bottom tier, wire the second layer into the basket frame.

**3** Next fill a plastic bowl with the blocks of soaked floral foam. Secure them into the liner with pot tape, then fit them snugly into the basket by placing sphagnum moss all around. Make sure that the floral foam is at least 2 inches above the edge of the container to create a rounded effect.

**4** Starting with the ivy berries, trim into branches of about 3 inches and place all around the basket at different heights, but all radiating from a central point. Then follow with the skimmia and American oak until you can hardly see the floral foam. By now you should have created a rounded structure into which you can put your flowers.

**5** First cut the holly berries into branches of 3 to 4 inches, place these around the arrangement, and then add the leucospermums and the textural rudbeckia. Finally add the two types of roses in groups of threes.

1

2

3

4

1

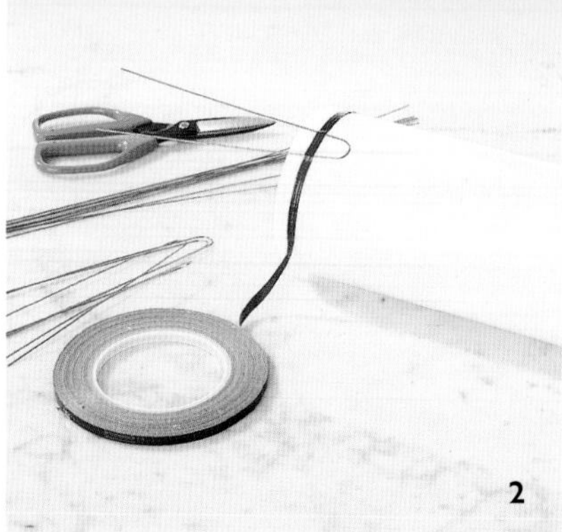

2

3

### you will need

- a roll of double-sided tape
- an 8-inch plastic pot
- heavy florists' wires
- a pot of *Calluna vulgaris* 'Silver Green'
- a roll of floral tape
- a pillar candle
- 2 blocks of floral foam
- 5 stems of *Brachyglottis* 'Sunshine'
- 5 stems of *Garrya elliptica*
- 5 stems of ivy
- a branch of *Alnus glutinosa*
- 3 *Brassica oleracea* 'White Crane'
- 3 stems of *Trachelium caeruleum* 'Lake Powell'
- 5 stems of *Hypericum* 'Jade'
- 3 stems of *Rosa* 'White Princess'
- 6 stems of *Rosa* 'Akito'
- 6 stems of *Rosa* 'Lemonade'
- 6 *Chrysanthemum* 'White Revert'

4

5

# natural container

This inexpensive way to conceal plastic containers gives any arrangement a modern look. There is something in the garden or on the market in every season that can be used effectively, and at little cost.

**1** Place a length of double-sided tape around the plastic pot. Cut little bunches of heather from the plant and stick them to the double-sided tape.

**2** Bend the heavy florists' wires into hairpins and tape onto the end of the candle.

**3** To secure the heather, place a wire or a ribbon around the bowl. Fill the bowl with the blocks of soaked floral foam. Make sure that the foam is at least 2 inches above the edge of the container by filling out the bottom with the ends of the block of foam. Trim the bottom of the wires on the candle, then place it firmly in the center of the foam so that the candle is well anchored.

**4** Use the foliage to cover the floral foam, making sure that it all radiates from a central point. Using at least three different types of foliage gives an interesting textural effect.

**5** Place the large-headed flowers into the arrangement first at different heights and depths around the bowl. Next add the hypericum cut up into small sprigs. Use the roses in groups to balance with the larger heavy flowers. Add the white chrysanthemum 'White Revert'.

# foam wreath

Floral foam rings are available in many different sizes. They are great for creating centerpieces, particularly when they are plastic backed. Small rings can sit on the arms at the top of candelabra. Larger rings can be used to create circles around the base of table candelabra.

## you will need

- a 12-inch foam ring in a plastic tray
- 2 bunches of galax
- 2 bunches of *Brachyglottis* 'Sunshine'
- at least 50 stems of sweet peas
- a pack of thin taper candles

**1** Soak the ring for five minutes in tepid water. If you have some flower food, place it into the bowl as well, as it will help feed the flowers and counteract any bacteria. Before adding any flowers, green up the ring with the foliage. I like to use plastic-backed wreath frames wherever possible and to edge the ring with large leaves. One of the easiest to use is galax. I find these to be just the right size and they also have tough stems that are easier to insert into the foam.

**2** After you have edged all around the ring, add the *Brachyglottis* at different angles, creating a lovely rounded effect.

**3** Finally add the sweet peas, working from one end of the ring to the other, taking care to put them in at different heights and depths around the frame. Sweet peas have very delicate stems, so it is vital that you hold your hand as near to the flower heads as possible and push them into the foam very carefully to avoid breaking their fragile stems. Finally, add the candles by pushing down firmly into the soaked foam.

**1**

**2**

**3**

# mossed wreath

Moss works like floral foam by holding water for the flowers and foliage to keep them alive. It is used when the plant material is heavy. Apples and cones would be too heavy to wire into foam, so this technique is one we return to every winter for our Christmas rings.

## you will need

- a bag of sphagnum moss
- a wire wreath ring
- a roll of strong wire
- a pair of scissors
- a bunch of blue pine
- 3 large and 10 small fir cones
- a selection of long, strong wire
- 10 small apples
- 5 dried limes and 10 orange slices
- a pack of long cinnamon sticks
- a bunch of mistletoe
- a bunch of holly sprigs
- a bunch of larch twigs
- a roll of ribbon

**1** Bind the sphagnum moss onto a wire wreath frame using heavy wire over and under the wire frame.

**2** Trim the moss with scissors, then begin to add the base of foliage. It is easier if you bind the foliage onto the frame rather than wire each individual sprig. Use three pieces for each section of the ring, one pointing inward, one outward, and one for the central area.

**3** Wire all your decorations with a heavy stub wire. For the cones, apples, dried limes, and orange slices, place a wire through the base of the item, then twist the two lengths of wire together.

**4** Wire the decorations, mistletoe, and holly sprigs in groups onto the frame, then add sprigs of larch to encircle the wreath and add movement. Pin the ribbon around the wreath so that it looks as though it is weaving in and out from the center towards the edge.

# wired boutonniere

Flowers and foliage are wired in a boutonniere to make it lighter than it would be on a natural stem and also to give it longevity. The thinner stalk, which is made from wire covered with green stem tape, helps to preserve the flower and makes it easier to pin onto a lapel.

1

2

## you will need

- a *Rosa* 'Alexis'
- a selection of wires
- a sprig of rosemary
- a branch of *Viburnum tinus*
- a branch of ivy
- a length of green stem tape
- a pearl-headed pin

**1** Select a well-formed rose and remove the stem just below the seed box. Insert a short stub wire into the stem and up into the seed box. Double-leg mount three sprigs of rosemary and two sprigs of *Viburnum tinus* flowers. To create a double-leg mount, make a hairpin bend with the wire and loop one wire over the other three times. Choose three good ivy leaves and stitch through the vein at the back. Take one leg over the other.

**2** Take a length of stem tape and stretch it so that you bind the wires together. This helps to keep the moisture in and softens the wires. Arrange three pieces of rosemary around the rose head and the two sprigs of *Viburnum tinus* berries, then edge with the three ivy leaves. Bind them all together with the stem tape, then trim the stem so that it is about 1 inch long. Add a pearl-headed pin so that the boutonniere can be secured onto clothing.

# wired napkin ring

This simple technique works particularly well with robust bell-shaped flowers, such as hyacinths or stephanotis pips. The same principle can be applied to other small flowers, such as daisies, but you will need to retain a small amount of stem otherwise too many flower heads are required.

1

## you will need

- a stem of *Hyacinthus orientalis* 'Minos'
- a reel of purple florists' wire
- a spool of ¼-inch ribbon

**1** Pull the individual pips off the hyacinth and thread them onto the length of purple wire so that they are all facing the same direction.

**2** When you have completed enough to bind the napkin, loop the two wires together, then trim the napkin with a looped ribbon bow.

# index

*Figures in italics refer to captions*

# acknowledgments

Thanks once again to all the Paula Pryke Flowers team especially Gina, Tania, Penny, Anne, Ann, Hisako, Sarah, Shontelle, Katie, Anita, Wendy, and Karen.

Thank you to Jacqui Small and all her team, especially Kerenza Swift. A huge thank you to Maggie Town who has had to work unbelievably hard on the design of this huge book against an impossible deadline! Thanks for making it look so good. Sian Parkhouse once again—despite all the odds—managed to get me to write the copy and edited it on time despite a shrinking deadline. Thank you, Sian, for all your comments and advice once more.

Thank you to all the talented photographers I have had the pleasure of working with who have contributed work to this book:

Sarah Cuttle
Pages 1, 4, 8, 17, 19 (except no. 3 and no. 4), 20–23 left, 24 top, 25, 26, 31 (except no. 1 and no. 2), 34, 35, 37 right, 39–41, 43, 45 (except no. 1), 48, 49, 54, 56–60, 63, 66 no.7, 70, 71, 77, 79, 83, 84, 86–92, 97 (except no. 2 and no. 4), 98, 100–104, 107, 188 (except no. 1 and no. 8), 118–21, 124–25, 135, 136, 140–42, 144, 147, 153, 158, 162, 164, 165, 168, 171, 174–83, 193, 195, 196, 198–205, 207, 209, 213–17, 220–23, 227, 229–31, 234–36, 241, 244–56, 258–260, 264, 265, 268–71, 274–77, 279–81, 285, 288–90, 292–95, 298, 300–11, 314–17, 320, 326, 334, 335, 340, 341, 354, 355–61, 374–77

Sian Irvine
Pages 2–3, 11, 12, 13, 14–15, 19 no. 3 and no. 4, 23 right, 24 bottom, 27, 28, 29, 31 no. 1 and no. 2, 36, 37 left, 38, 42, 45 no.1, 50–51, 52, 55, 61, 78, 93, 97 no. 2 and no. 4, 105, 106, 108, 109, 110–11, 188 no. 1 and no. 8, 116, 117, 122, 123, 128–9, 130–34, 137–39, 143, 145, 146, 150–52, 154, 155, 166–70, 172, 173, 184–85, 187, 190–92, 194, 197, 206, 208, 212, 218, 219, 224–25, 232, 237–39, 257, 266, 267, 291, 299, 312–13, 321, 322, 328, 329, 342–54, 362–73, 378–81

David Loftus
Pages 18, 30, 44, 64, 82, 96, 112, 156, 157

Chris Tubbs
Pages 32, 33, 46, 47, 53, 67, 68, 69, 85, 94, 95, 99, 114, 115, 261, 262, 263, 324, 325, 336–33

Polly Wreford
Pages 5, 7, 10, 62, 65, 66 (except no. 7), 69, 72–76, 80, 81, 127, 148, 149, 159–61, 163, 188–89, 210, 211, 233, 240, 242–43, 273, 278, 282–84, 286, 287, 296, 297, 318, 319, 323, 327, 330–31, 333

www.paula-pryke-flowers.com